ALTERNATE ASSESSMENT OF STUDENTS WITH SIGNIFICANT COGNITIVE DISABILITIES

ALTERNATE ASSESSMENT OF STUDENTS WITH SIGNIFICANT COGNITIVE DISABILITIES

A Research Report

Dr. Icylin Leslie Harding

Copyright © 2016 by Dr. Icylin Leslie Harding.

Library of Congress Control Number:		2016911655
ISBN:	Hardcover	978-1-5245-2599-6
	Softcover	978-1-5245-2598-9
	eBook	978-1-5245-2597-2

All rights reserved. No part of this book may be reproduced or transmitted in any form or by any means, electronic or mechanical, including photocopying, recording, or by any information storage and retrieval system, without permission in writing from the copyright owner.

Any people depicted in stock imagery provided by Thinkstock are models, and such images are being used for illustrative purposes only.
Certain stock imagery © Thinkstock.

Print information available on the last page.

Rev. date: 09/09/2016

To order additional copies of this book, contact:
Xlibris
1-888-795-4274
www.Xlibris.com
Orders@Xlibris.com
736655

The education system continues to face challenges to use the right strategies for both instruction and assessment of students. It is no wonder why Dr. Harding, after spending many years as a teacher with both 'regular' students and students with significant cognitive disabilities has decided to investigate the relationship between teacher preparation and administering alternate assessment. Assessing students is a very critical aspect of educating students . It is definitely a mammoth task because 'one shoe' does not fit all. Dr. Harding has been very strong on the subject with the intention to capture the curious minds of educators who share her concerns that we must continue seek to be highly qualified to serve our student in this 21st century.

Thelma Lewis

Over the past decade, educational assessment has become essential for holding schools accountable for teaching all students. This research highlights the need for continuous training of teachers in how to incorporate alternate assessment in their daily instruction to ensure that students with significant cognitive disabilities assess the general curriculum in meaningful ways.

Dr. Sandra Martin

This research book is an exceptional resource for special education teachers or anyone who is interested in assessing students with significant cognitive disabilities. There is a wealth of information contained in this book that is based on extensive research and professional experience. The information found in this book is timely and pertinent at a time when there is a need for special education teachers who can effectively administer alternate assessments to students with significant cognitive disabilities.
Dr. Harding's book examines the relationship between teacher preparation, teacher experience and teacher attitude in administering alternate assessment to students with significant cognitive disabilities.

Based on the findings, the writer offers suggestions for educators in the area of special education to develop and share best practices in developing and administering the alternate assessment.

Joy Taylor-Roberts

I have known Dr. Icylin Harding for more than 40 years. It is with great pleasure that I write in support of her attempt to publish her book. Her record of continuous achievement as a teacher warrants this accomplishment. The information she provided in her work could greatly assist teachers in becoming more prepared in administering alternative assessments to cognitively challenged students.

Dr. Harding constantly strives for excellent and works diligently to help others. Her qualification and experiences are impressive and I believe she has represented her community very well.

Dr. Linette L. Leslie-Fondon

For many years assessing students especially those who are cognitively challenged has been a hot topic among educators. Dr. Harding, a dedicated and passionate educator, who has taught student with disability for many years, is no stranger to this issue. Therefore, it is on this premise she took on the challenge to research the relationship between teacher preparation and administering alternate assessments. As a fellow educator, I certainly thank and endorse Dr. Harding on the findings and the positive lead that she has taken to stir other educators to continue to seek and implement other methods of instructing and assessing both to regular and special needs students.

Claudia Wynter-McKay

CONTENTS

Acknowledgments xix
Foreword.. xxi
    Teachers' Challenges in Administering Alternative
    Assessment xxi
Chapter 1: The Problem 1
    Problem Background 2
    Theoretical Framework 5
    Problem Statement 6
    Purpose of the Study 7
    Research Questions 8
    Limitations of the Study 8
    Delimitations of Study 8
    Definition of Terms 9
    Significance of Study 10
    Summary 10
Chapter 2: Review of the Literature 12
    The Historical Perspective of the Legal Framework
    Governing Alternate Assessments 12
    Historical Overview of Georgia's Implementation of
    the Alternate Assessment 16
    Approaches to Alternate Assessment 17
    Portfolio-Based Assessment 25

> Teacher Preparation...27
> Factors Influencing Teacher Attitudes..................................34
> Teacher Experience 36
> Summary 37

Chapter 3: Methodology...38
> Research Design 39
> Instrumentation..42
> Pilot Study...43
> Data-Collection Procedures 43
> Assumptions..44
> Data Analysis 44
> Summary 47

Chapter 4: Findings 49
> Restatement of the Purpose...49
> Pilot Study...49
> Research Question 1..50
> Research Question 2..54
> Thematic Extractions from Question 1 and Question 2 59
> Theme 1: Teacher attitude played an important role in the administration of the Georgia Alternate Assessment...........59
> Theme 2: Teacher experience is not a crucial factor................59
> Research Question 3..60
> Thematic Extractions 61
> *Theme 1: Formal education had little influence on administering the Georgia Alternate 61*
> *Assessment. 61*
> Theme 2: Differing perceived value in training. 64

    Theme 3: Unfamiliarity with curriculum and Georgia Alternate Assessment. 67

    Conclusion 70

Chapter 5: Study, Summary, and Recommendations 72

    Conclusion 76

    Research Question 1 76

    Research Question 2 77

    Research Question 3 77

    Implications for Practice 78

    Implications for Research 79

    Recommendations 79

References 81

Appendixes

Appendix A: Permission to Use Survey Tool 93

Appendix B: County Permission to Use Facilities 95

Appendix C: IRB Approval 96

Appendix D: Principal Permission to Use Facilities 98

Appendix E: Letter of Invitation 100

Appendix F: Informed Consent for Participants Age 18 and Older 101

Appendix G: Alternate Assessment Impact Survey 105

Appendix H: Open-Ended Questionnaire 108

Tables

Table 1. Alternate assessment systems used in different states ... 17

Table 2. The attitudes of elementary school teachers on how to administer the alternate assessment 51

Table 3. The attitudes of middle school teachers on how to administer the alternate assessment 52

Table 4. The attitudes of high school teachers on how to administer the alternate assessment 53

Table 5. Teaching experience and teacher attitude 1 54

Table 6. Teaching experience and teacher attitude 2 54

Table 7. Teaching experience and teacher attitude 3 55

Table 8. Teaching experience and teacher attitude 4 55

Table 9. Teaching experience and teacher attitude 5 55

Table 10. Teaching experience and teacher attitude 6 56

Table 11. Teaching experience and teacher attitude 7 56

Table 12. Teaching experience and teacher attitude 8 56

Table 13. Teaching experience and teacher attitude 9 57

Table 14. Teaching experience and teacher attitude 10 57

Table 15. Teaching experience and teacher attitude 11 57

Table 16. Teaching experience and teacher attitude 12 58

Table 17. Teaching experience and teacher attitude 13 58

Table 18. Teaching experience and teacher attitude 14 58

Table 19. Teaching experience and teacher attitude 15 59

Table 20. The composition of teacher participants at school level 60

Figures

Figure 1: School District Demographics 40
Figure 2: Demographics of Participants 41

The purpose of this descriptive study was to examine the relationship between teacher preparation, teacher experience, and teacher attitude, in administering alternate assessment to students with significant cognitive disabilities. The study used a purposive and convenient sampling of forty-two participants currently administering GAA to students with significant cognitive disabilities in one school district. Teacher experience had limited influence on the attitude of teachers in administering the alternate assessment. Teacher preparation, training, and staff development were the main methods of preparing teachers for administering the alternate assessment, rather than college experience and education. Based on the findings, the researcher suggested the creation of collaborative and continuous opportunities for special education teachers to develop and share best practices in administering the alternate assessment.

To all committed special education teachers working with students with significant cognitive disability.

The idea of publishing this book was generated from the urge to share information gleaned from this study with policy makers, educators, parents and the community as a whole. However, I was further propelled to do so by the encouragement of close colleagues who thought the study was excellent, informative and appealing. Also, after several years' experience of working with teachers and assessing students with significant cognitive disabilities, my observation is that many teachers are challenged using the alternate assessment technique for varying reasons. Hence, the publishing of "The Impact of Pedagogical Attitude on Alternate Assessment of Students with Significant Cognitive Disabilities."

ACKNOWLEDGMENTS

I would like to express sincere gratitude to Dr. Joseph Balloun, chairperson of my graduate committee, for his guidance and assistance. Thank you for your patience and encouragement throughout this journey. Thanks to my committee members, Dr. Victoria Landu and Dr. Addie Davis, for your invaluable support and guidance in the planning and implementation of this research project. Special thanks to Dr. Jeannette Dubyak for the assistance given during the dissertation process. I wish to thank my cousin Thelma Lewis for your prayer and support. A special thanks to Dr. Carlene Graham for reading and giving valuable suggestions. Thanks to my friend and colleague Dr. Joy Taylor-Roberts for being optimistic even during challenging times.

The deepest appreciation is further offered to administrators, principals, special education coordinators, and special education teachers of the school system that participated in this research study. Thank you for the warm welcome extended when I visited your board of education office and schools. I am deeply grateful to all the teachers who used valuable time to complete the surveys. Without these contributions, this study would not have been possible.

FOREWORD

Teachers' Challenges in Administering Alternative Assessment

I was privileged to serve as chair for Dr. Icylin Harding's dissertation. She has years of extensive hands-on experience with the challenges in meeting the needs of special education students. From her background, she recognized and addressed a difficult and timely problem. Her research shows a continuing need for improved training of teachers who do alternative assessments for special education students.

The public schools are responsible for meeting the academic needs of all students, including those with significant disabilities. Students in the general K-12 education population are educated in a common curriculum. The assessment of their academic skills is typically a group evaluation designed to match assessment with the common curriculum content.

Special education students are diverse, and are taught in small groups or individually with specific, individualized and functional goals besides some content taught to the general student population. The special education eligibilities include, for example, autism, hearing or visually impaired, speech-language disabilities, behavioral and emotional problems, specific learning disabilities, and mild, moderate, severe and profound cognitive disabilities. The assessments used for students in the general population usually are inappropriate for students with severe disabilities.

Special education teachers of students with severe disabilities are required to do alternative assessments of individual students on a yearly basis. There is general agreement in the literature that special education teachers need more help to become proficient in alternative assessments. However, a programmatic needs assessment should be done before designing a program meant to help special education teachers do an even better job in alternative assessments. Dr. Harding investigated the teachers' self-reported needs for guidance in how to do alternative assessment. Dr. Harding also developed specific recommendations for how to improve training in alternative assessment from those who face the problem every day. Her recommendations will lead to more relevant and consistent preparation of special education teachers to do alternative assessments.

Joseph Balloun Ph.D.,
Industrial and Organizational Psychology
Mercer University

CHAPTER 1

The Problem

In today's educational climate, there are increasing demands of accountability for improved student achievement. The responsibility of preparing teachers to meet the demands of the realities of today's classroom is a difficult and challenging endeavor. Teacher educators, teachers, and school systems are now acknowledging the need to implement instructional and assessment practices that both inform and improve teacher practices, student learning, and subsequently, student academic advancement (British Columbia, Ministry of Education 2005). To this end, it promotes the development of educational practices in the classroom that integrate specific strategies and alternate assessment tools that lead to enhanced student achievement. The difficulties and challenges are, in most part, due to the diverse cultural backgrounds, nationalities, and languages of the students in the classroom. Above all, students with significant cognitive disabilities create the greatest challenge for the classroom teacher (Zatta 2003).

The passage of No Child Left Behind (NCLB 2002) and the 1997 Individuals with Disabilities Education Act (IDEA) created the beginning of the high-stakes accountability movement. This dramatic movement in education brought a set of essential legal protections under IDEA (1997). The IDEA provides eligible students with equal access to public education as given to regular education students while making public schools responsible to meet the academic needs of students with significant disabilities (Digest of Education Statistics 2005). However, Jones (2004) contended that although these efforts are commendable, the federal laws exclude mandating the preparation or training of special education teachers to meet these demands. It is now even more imperative that teachers are capable of efficiently instructing and assessing all students, inclusive of students qualifying for alternate assessments (Browder, Davis, and Karovenen 2005).

Of the 49.5 million general education students in the United States, almost 14 percent, or 6.6 million, of this nation's school-age children receive some level of additional assistance through special education (26th Annual Report to Congress, June 2007). These children represent all races and ethnic groups and speak several different languages. The representation of race/ethnicity is as follows: white–59.5 percent, black–20.5 percent, Hispanic–16.6 percent, Indian/Alaska native–2.0 percent, and Asian/Pacific–1.4 percent. Many of these students receive services through Title I and English language services, in addition to special education (26th Annual Report to Congress 2007). It is interesting to note the vast differences existing across states concerning the percent of students in receipt of special education. For example, in the 2003–2004 school year, states varied from a low of 10.5 percent in California to a high of 20.2 percent in Rhode Island (Digest of Education Statistics 2005).

Naturally, students with significant cognitive disabilities perform poorly on the state standardized tests taken by the typical student (IDEA 1997). Failure is partly due to students being cognitively unable to participate in the test. For the first time, students with significant cognitive disabilities have the opportunity to demonstrate actual abilities through mandated standard-driven education. States and school systems responded to the federal mandate by implementing alternate assessments as a measure of academic accountability for students with significant disabilities (IDEA 2001).

Problem Background

The 2001 reauthorization of the Elementary and Secondary Education Act (ESEA), known as NCLB, brought about an impressive change in the intensity of attention given to the millions of public school students identified as significantly disabled. Historically, these students perform poorly in school (26th Annual Report to Congress, June 2007). Because the disabilities interfere with the students' central processing capabilities, many students in the United States identified as significantly disabled are struggling or failing academically (Browder, Karovenen, and Davis 2005). However, educators, psychologists, and others attempt to work around the deficiency and expose these students to learning and assessment (Zatta 2003). Of note, Farrington (2003) pointed out that between 3 and 4 million people between the ages of six and twenty-two years acknowledged having some type of learning disability.

Although only a mere 1 to 2 percent of students are involved in alternate assessment, this is a high-priority educational initiative resulting from federal mandates for the accountability of academic progress of students with significant cognitive disabilities alongside regular education students (Jones 2004). Since 2000, there is a growing trend toward the implementation of alternate assessment as each state identifies alternate methods of assessing students with significant disabilities as a means of satisfying federal and state mandates (Browder, Karovenen, and Davis 2005; Kamper, Horvath, Kleinert, and Farmer-Kearns 2001; Jones 2004). As more states and school systems adopt the trend of implementing alternate assessment, the greater the demands for adequately prepared teachers are. Browder et al. and Hughes (2006) suggested that a gap existed in this area of research, adding that to date, there were few studies examining the relationship between teacher preparedness, teacher attitude, and teacher experience toward administering the alternate assessment.

By implementing a portfolio-based alternate assessment program, the state of Georgia has responded to the changing environment in assessment by exposing students with significant disabilities to alternate assessment based on academic standards (Georgia Department of Education [GaDOE] 2007). In the 2006–2007 session of the Georgia Alternate Assessment (GAA), just fewer than ten thousand students participated in the GAA in reading/language arts, mathematics, science, and social studies (GaDOE).

In a study conducted with teachers in an urban district within a high-stakes accountability state, the findings indicated that student performance on the alternate assessments was more likely to improve when teacher preparation included acquiring skills to apply varying instructional and assessment approaches (Browder, Karvonen, Davis, Fallin, and Courtade-Little 2005). The researchers recommended more studies in this area for further confirmation.

Ysseldyke, Dennison, and Nelson (2003) found that having students with significant cognitive disabilities mandatorily participating in the alternate assessment was a way to pioneer advanced academic expectations. This higher expectation subsequently sets the spotlight on achievement in the planning of individualized education program (IEP) of students with significant cognitive disabilities (Ysseldyke et al.).

Kentucky began restructuring alternate assessment with the passing of the Kentucky Reform Education Act I of 1972 (Kamper et al. 2001). Over the last ten years, all students in Kentucky, including students with intellectual disabilities, participated in assessment and earned scores based on performance. As each state implements its individual alternate assessment program and guidelines, a deliberate effort for evaluation and efficiency must be included (Kamper et al. 2001). States must consider reliable, economical, and unbiased instruments for assessment. In the case of Georgia, reliability is established when a minimum of two raters of the portfolio tend to agree highly with each other on student performance (GaDOE). With this and other factors in place, some states are also failing to recognize the importance of having well-prepared teachers in place prior to the implementation of alternate assessments (Hughes 2006).

On a national level, the current body of knowledge on alternate assessment is new as well as limited (Browder, Spooner, Algozzine, et al. 2003). Further research is necessary in all areas of teacher preparation in relationship to teachers administering alternate assessment (Browder et al.). To date, no study has investigated the relationship between teacher preparation, teacher experience, and teacher attitude toward administering alternate assessment (Browder et al.).

Noll (2006) posited that exceptional education teachers, already overtaxed, are required to accept the responsibilities of administering alternate assessments without adequate teacher preparation. Browder et al. (2005), Hughes (2006), and Zatta (2003) concluded that teacher preparation was significant to administering alternate assessments. The changing approaches to instruction and alternate assessment require teacher educators to seek diverse approaches to prepare all teachers, including special education teachers, to meet these demands (Hughes 2006; Perry and Power 2004; Kamper et al.).

Increased dissatisfaction with nonaccountability of the academic progress of students with significant cognitive disabilities, coupled with the lack of teacher preparation by colleges and universities for administering alternate assessments, reflect the state of public education (Hughes 2006). Understanding the needs of students with significant cognitive disabilities will allow colleges, universities, and school systems to acknowledge responsibility for preparing teachers to cope with the various instructional and assessment needs of all students in the classroom (Hughes 2006).

Theoretical Framework

Bruner's (1997) theory on conceptual change suggested that teacher preparation becomes more meaningful when the theory is connected to its application. Bruner added, "Teaching specific topics or skills without making the context clear in the broader fundamental structure of a field of knowledge is uneconomical" (p. 31). Theories should not be taught in a "vacuum" but ought to help teachers understand the relatedness between the ideas taught and the anticipated real classroom applications (Hughes 2006).

Gardner's theory on multiple intelligences (MI) uniquely points out the deficiencies in the classroom, whereby students with significant cognitive disabilities are not exposed enough to the kinesthetic and visual arts and domestic activities. Exposure to such activities awakens as many of the intelligences as possible (Gardner 1993).

Dewey's (1959) constructivist theory on experience contended that teaching and learning are uninterrupted processes of experience. Additionally, Dewey determined that experience was an interactive process between human beings and the surroundings. "The value of the experience is to be judged by the effect that experience has on the individual's present, future, and the extent to which the individual is able to contribute to society" (Dewey 1959, 29).

Dewey's philosophy of attitude suggested that one's attitudes, beliefs, and experience affect the educator's contribution and the learner's outcome. Experience influences one's attitudes toward accepting or rejecting change. A teacher's attitude, be it negative or positive, is sensed by the entire environment and influences the atmosphere of change, including student learning (Dewey 1959).

Banks (2006) supported the idea that successful teacher preparation encompasses training teachers to understand laws governing education, ethnicity, cultural diversity, and acceptance of all students regardless of disabilities. Teacher preparation must include assisting teachers to develop the ability to work cooperatively with administrators and other professionals. This is critical and shores up the theory that a well-prepared and perceptive teacher must work within a supportive institutional setting to succeed at meeting students' academic and other demands (Banks).

Ysseldyke, Dennison, and Nelson (2003) contended that although there is a protracted history of assessment-based accountability, hard data on the relationship between teacher preparedness for administering alternate assessment of students with significant cognitive disabilities was sparse. In addition, there was no empirical evidence to reflect the role of teachers in this initiative. In terms of training, Browder, Karvonen, Davis, Fallin, and Courtade-Little (2005) suggested that research was required to discover the kinds of training, professional development, and new resources that teachers required to teach and assess students with cognitive disabilities.

Problem Statement

Special education teachers are mandated to administer alternate assessment; however, little is known about teacher preparation, experience, and attitude in administering the assessment as mandated by the NCLB/IDEA laws (Hughes 2006). Hughes contended that preparing teachers for the realities of today's classroom was a challenging endeavor. These difficulties and challenges were partly due to the diverse cultural backgrounds, nationalities, and languages of the students in the classroom. Above all, students with significant cognitive disabilities create the greatest challenge for the classroom teacher (Jones 2004).

While IDEA (1997) has placed new challenges on states and school systems to implement alternate assessment for accounting for the academic progress of students with significant cognitive disabilities, these federal mandates have neglected to include the preparation of teachers as an essential part of the equation to meet these stipulations (Hughes 2006). In addition, colleges, universities, and school systems are failing to prepare teachers adequately for the task of coping with instructional and assessment demands initiated by federal laws on education (Zatta 2003).

Teachers lacked preparation in understanding the implication of the federal mandates in relationship to alternate assessment and students with significant cognitive disabilities. For example, in 1993, noncompliance with IDEA law forced the State of Georgia Compliance Review Team to threaten to pull state and federal funding from one middle school in Georgia for failure to provide adequate services to students with significant disabilities (Jones 2004). Teachers also lacked preparation in learning how to transition from an independent living curriculum to a grade-level content curriculum (Browder et al. 2005; Quenemoen, Thompson, and Thurlow 2003). Hence, the need for further research on teacher preparation and teacher attitude in relationship to skills required for instruction in transitioning from one curriculum to the other. Effective preparation of teachers with positive attitude toward alternate assessment is crucial since both the school district and the state depend on the students' high performance to make adequate yearly progress (AYP).

Purpose of the Study

This descriptive study sought to examine the relationship between teacher preparation, teacher experience, teacher attitude, and administering alternate assessment to students with cognitive disabilities. This study examined whether teacher preparation, teacher experience, and teacher attitude influenced the administering of alternate assessment. Research investigating this area of administering alternate assessment is limited especially in Georgia, where the GAA was implemented in the 2006–2007 school year. Three research questions were used to guide this concurrent mixed-methods study design to explore the results in detail.

Research Questions

This study addressed the following questions:

RQ1. What is the relationship between individual teacher's attitude in administering the alternate assessment?
RQ2. Is there a relationship between teacher experiences and attitude in administering the alternate assessment?
RQ3. How has teacher preparation influenced the administering of alternate assessment?

A survey utilizing the Likert scale was used to collect data. Responses to question 1 assisted in determining any correlation between teacher attitude and how the teacher actually administered the alternate assessment. Question 2 allowed for exploration of how teacher experience influenced the attitude of teachers administering the alternate assessment. The responses to question 3 collected through an open-ended questionnaire assisted in examining and describing how teacher preparation influenced the administration of alternate assessment.

Limitations of the Study

The study was limited to the number of surveys completed and returned. The level of honesty displayed by teachers when responding to the questionnaire and survey offered other limitations.

Delimitations of Study

This study was delimited to one suburban school district in the Southeastern United States. The sample population included only special education teachers in one suburban school district.

Definition of Terms

Terms used in the study were the following:

accountability: An extensive attempt throughout the United States to hold state and school district responsible for all students' academic progress (Zatta 2003).

administering alternate assessment: Is defined as a way of measuring nonstandardized assessment to students who are incapable of participating in the general assessment (GaDOE 2008).

alternate assessment: Alternate assessment is a substitute form of collecting data on the academic performance of students with significant disabilities (Ysseldyke, Olsen, and Thurlow 1997).

alternate assessment teacher survey: Instrument used to investigate the relationship between teacher preparation, teacher experience, teacher attitude, and administering alternate assessment.

authentic assessment: A form of assessment used to evaluate students' knowledge and abilities of real-world activities through assignments and projects related to the classroom curriculum (Klienert and Kearns 2001).

Georgia Alternate Assessment (GAA): The GAA is a portfolio-based assessment of student work providing evidence that the student is making progress toward grade-level academic standards (GaDOE 2006).

IDEA (Individuals with Disabilities Education Act of 1997): The name of the law passed, mandating school personnel to include students with disabilities as part of the assessment for yearly academic progress (IDEA 1997).

individual with significant disabilities: Students whose cognitive ability falls within either the severe or the profound level of retardation with at least one or more additional disabilities (Zatta 2003).

individualized education program: An individualized education plan designed to meet the unique educational needs of a student with significant disabilities (Browder et al. 2006).

performance assessment: A form of testing that requires a student to construct a response or a product that shows the student's abilities and skills (GaDOE 2007).

portfolio-based assessment: Performance-based collection of samples of student work that demonstrate student's progress and performance in different areas (Klienert and Kearns 2001).

relationship: The state of being related or interrelated (between variables) (Moore 2006).

teacher attitude: The way the teacher looks at life influences the thinking toward instruction and learning in the classroom (Dewey 1959).

teacher experience: Refers to knowledge and skills gained by teaching over time (Browder 2006).

teacher preparation: To train teachers to impart knowledge and skills that enhance student learning (Browder, Karovenen, and Davis 2005).

For the purposes of this study, teacher preparation related to training teachers to administer alternate assessments, to teach academic content on grade-level, and to be knowledgeable of the legal framework relating to alternate assessment for students with significant cognitive disabilities.

Significance of Study

Findings from the study may provide important information for the college and university departments of education to support the advanced teacher preparation programs for alternate assessment. The new approach to training may reflect teachers' needs, as well as satisfy federal mandates. Additionally, the study may contribute to the knowledge available to school systems that will subsequently improve ongoing professional development for teachers in public school.

Summary

The research study has five chapters. Chapter 1 offered the setting of the study, the research problem statement, and the research questions that provided the focal point of this study. Chapter 2 interpreted the results of the significant literature connected to the level of teacher preparation and teacher attitude necessary to successfully implement alternate assessments. Chapter 3 described the setting of the study and the research methodology. Chapter 4 discussed the findings of the study, while in chapter 5, conclusion were drawn from the findings as illustrated in chapter 4, along with inferences drawn for research implications and recommendations.

CHAPTER 2

Review of the Literature

Chapter 2 identified pertinent literature relevant to the study. The literature review consists of four major components. These include a historical perspective of the legal framework governing alternate assessment, portfolio-based alternate assessment, the impact of teacher preparation on alternate assessment scores, and teacher training model.

The Historical Perspective of the Legal Framework Governing Alternate Assessments

This report demonstrated the inevitability of establishing an education framework to satisfy the requirements of all students combined. The 1980s decisions on educational reform were representative of "top-down" efforts to introduce planned changes. As a result, these changes were unsuccessful in bringing about meaningful changes in instruction and academic advancement. The splintered and ambiguous policies sidetracked teachers' concentration while not providing the quality of professional support required to improve teaching methods (Center for Policy Research 1996, 3). The failure at the initial attempt at education reform led to the beginning of a methodical approach to education reform in the United States (US).

In 1989, President George Bush and the country's governors organized an education summit that piloted the approval of six education goals deemed to succeed by year 2000. The six plus two additional goals became the Goals 2000: Educate America Act (PL 103–227). In 1994, there was an enactment of the policy materialized under President Clinton's administration. The expectation of Goals 2000 stated, "All children can learn and achieve to high standards, and must realize true potential if the United States is to prosper" (PL 103–227, section 301 [1]). The mandate further suggested that every child must participate in an extensive and challenging curriculum, and that adequate resources be made available for these and other educational demands (McDonnell, McLaughlin, and Morison 1997). Florian and Pullin (2000) postulated that the legislation proposed to introduce advanced levels of academic possibilities to improve US economic competitiveness with other countries. Goal 2000 became noteworthy because it was the first piece of legislation directly intended for regular education students but mandated the inclusion of students with disabilities within the framework for education reform. The most significant matter targeted in the methodical educational restructuring was the start of an educational system that had similar expectations from both special and general education students.

The 1997 reauthorization of Individuals with Disabilities Education Act (IDEA) also mandated the inclusion of students with disabilities in the education reform proposals. IDEA supported the federal mandate for a free appropriate public education within the least restrictive environment and safeguards for the rights of children and families of children with disabilities. The IDEA further mandated local school systems and states to develop and implement practices for providing complete educational prospects for students with disabilities. The changes in IDEA came about from congressional findings, which stated that students with disabilities must access the regular curriculum (NCLB 2001).

Over the last thirty years, there has been a worldwide increase in the use of criterion-referenced assessment (Yovanoff and Tindal 2007). However, the history of the use of alternate assessments for extensive district-wide or statewide testing is short and persuasive. Passage of the Individuals with Disabilities Act 1997 established the requirement for alternate assessments to facilitate students with significant disabilities engaging in the large-scale testing programs. These alternate assessments were nonspecific both in design and in focus. The empirical support for alternate assessment for this population of students was and continues to be debatable (Ysseldyke and Olsen 1997).

Yovanoff and Tindal (2007) examined the transition that focused on the assessment of students with significant disabilities over a thirty-year period. The study distinguished four major segments of intervention research and its impact on student assessment. In the early 1960s, programs that aligned with young children and childhood developmental theories used age-based practices. During the second phase in the late 1970s, functional curriculum in the domains of vocational, school, community, and recreation received the spotlight. A third phase surfaced in the 1990s, comprising the functional approach (balancing school and community access) with focus on school-based activities to concentrate on self-determination and independent living. Lastly, the drastic change came about with the passing of the Individuals with Disabilities Act of 1997 (IDEA). The fourth (last) segment was clearly academic oriented, focusing on academic standards.

The implementation of the IDEA brought three academic reaction formats for using alternate assessment: performance assessments, observations, and portfolios. These assessments have been undergoing psychometric appraisal (Messick 1996; Traub and Fisher 1977; Thissen, Wainer, and Wang 1994). If cautiously utilized, these forms of assessments emerge as part of the statewide or district-wide alternate assessment program (Yovanoff and Tindal 2007). Very few states use performance assessments that mirror the traditional type of standardized testing. Tindal (2005) argued that with this form of assessment, the teacher administered a basic number of tasks to the student and mark for accuracy.

Tindal (2005) suggested some ways for measuring such exercises in relationship to students with significant disabilities. For instance, teachers may choose a specific behavior characterizing a student's need, observe it in a practical setting, then score student's responses based on established rubric. Several states use observations as a way of assessing students with significant disabilities. For portfolios, teachers assemble samples of students' work based on criteria established by state and/or school systems (Ford, Davern, and Schnorr 2001). Teachers are equipped with state standards from which to choose relevant areas of the standards, followed by directions on how to assemble a portfolio for presentation. The level of modification of instructional techniques seen in the classroom depends on the expertise, skills, abilities, and preparation of individual teachers.

Yovanoff and Tindal (2007) suggested that the method of transforming standards and assessment established for regular education students was difficult for practical use by students with significant disabilities. The method of transformation must include a theory on purpose, coupled with measurement, and a course of action befitting the group of students to be serviced. Each state may choose one of two approaches in the attempt to create alternate assessment pointers: (1) make regular standards more manageable until an appropriate solution is found, or (2) remodel the regular education curriculum standards to resemble forms of functional skills (Yovanoff and Tindal; Ford, Davern, and Schnorr 2001, 213).

Over the last few decades, several waves of education reform have created changes in the public education system. The most significant of these changes include the standards-based education reform mandating greater accountability, inclusive of the NCLB Act of 2001. Because of these changes, all students are now being assessed on state content standards and are accountable to these standards regardless of disabilities even though at modified levels. However, even with the federal mandates, some students may not benefit academically from these laws because of the severe disabilities. All states ought to create alternate assessment programs that address student accountability and must comply with guidelines established in NCLB mandates.

Alternate assessment is a development in the making that is quite unlike normal assessments. The underlying theory and procedure is a continuous debate. Browder, Thurlow, et al. (2007) contended that there is disagreement about the level of influence of alternate assessment on academic learning of students with disabilities. The disagreement concerned the development, administering, and tallying scores of alternate assessment to make an impact on academic learning of students with disabilities (Browder et al. 2006). Expectations were that the process of developing alternate assessment would improve over time. Thompson and Thurlow (2003) and Browder et al. (2006) supported the view that the value of a student's results was not reliant on comparisons with other students' results. However, the importance of the alternate assessment was to know what each student is capable of accomplishing based on the established performance criterion.

Historical Overview of Georgia's Implementation of the Alternate Assessment

Federal mandates govern the state of Georgia's educational policies. Historically, the 1997 IDEA required that all students are included in assessments for the first time. This included students with significant cognitive disabilities. All states were mandated to develop alternate assessment for students with significant cognitive disabilities (GaDOE 2006).

The Georgia Department of Education worked with stakeholders to develop the first GAA that was implemented in 2000 (GaDOE 2007). This initiative failed to meet several of the federal mandates initiated by IDEA and NCLB. These legal mandates stipulated that all students have access to the general curriculum and are assessed on the progress toward achieving the set standards. Both the NCLB and IDEA authorized students with significant cognitive disabilities to participate in alternate assessment based on alternate standards. Access to the general curriculum may mirror prerequisite skills instead of grade-level skills. These standards must be challenging for students with significant disabilities and demonstrate a means of supporting individual academic growth in content and across all grades (GaDOE).

The new GAA is portfolio-based. Student work provides evidence that the student is making progress toward grade-level academic standards. The students' portfolios are the proven evidence of alignment with instructional actions and must be flexible to facilitate the multiplicity of the students taking part (GaDOE 2007). Grades K–2 will develop a portfolio in math and reading/language arts, while grades 3–8 and 11 will develop the portfolio in language arts/reading, science, social studies, and math. There are two collection periods during the school year. GaDOE continues to support the GAA (portfolio-based) as an appropriate assessment for students with significant cognitive disabilities. GAA is guided by the state curriculum standards and supported by the IEP team (GaDOE).

GaDOE Division of Exceptional Students/Assessment developed and implemented training workshops for teachers and other school personnel on the GAA. Some two thousand teachers of students with disabilities accessed training on how to align instruction to standards in compliance with state and federal mandates (GaDOE 2006). Teachers are required to apply instructional skills to align standards and develop instructional strategies to meet the academic requirements of this population of students (GaDOE and Webb 2002). Georgia implemented the new GAA in the 2006–2007 school year with just fewer than ten thousand students participating (GaDOE 2007).

Approaches to Alternate Assessment

The findings of past research suggested that there were several approaches to measurement available for use in an alternate assessment system (Yovanoff and Tindal 2007). States are using different approaches to alternate assessment. Thompson and Thurlow (2003) reported the following about the approaches taken by different states:

Table 1. Alternate assessment systems used in different states

Portfolio or body of proof	23 states
Analyzing IEPs	4 states
Checklist	15 states
Performance assessment	5 states
Developing and revising	3 states

This information indicated the frequency of each approach by different states. However, these approaches are not as specific and unmistakably described as it seems. For example, according to Thompson and Thurlow (2003), the states using the checklist approach and the states analyzing IEPs need a body of proof to verify scores assigned to students.

Regardless of the method of alternate assessment used, the district or state must combine its accountability system to generate an overall approximate result of achievement for all students participating in the alternate assessment. Therefore, whatever approach or method meets the requirement of the state or school system, it must evaluate the elements of specific standards in order to collate the data of students participating in the alternate assessment (Thompson and Thurlow 2003).

Although each state chooses different approaches, the alternate assessment must satisfy the federal mandate reporting obligations. In criticizing the purpose of alternate assessment, Thompson, Quenemoen, and Thurlow (2003) argued that if the main reason for implementing alternate assessments bordered around satisfying a federal authorization, educators would be losing a significant chance of enhancing learning opportunities for students with significant cognitive disabilities. States and school systems must be cognizant of the fact that alternate assessments only become effective and meaningful when the process included a comprehensible summary of students' ability to complete tasks in different situations and embodied definite links to constant and differentiated instruction and supervision for continued improvement (Thompson et al.).

When choosing an approach, each state must be aware of the issues that meet the requirement during the process of mapping out the plan for alternate assessment. One such critical issue is agreeing on a set of scales between individualization and standardization (Thompson et al. 2003). However, because of the diverse population involved in alternate assessment, the test must cater to a wide range of performance levels and rates to produce meaningful scores. Browder, Karvonen, et al. (2007) supported the view that if testing practices and conditions are not standardized, the disparity in results may have the following consequences: (1) differences in testing practices and conditions, (2) variations in students' capabilities, or (3) a mixture of these two issues. Standardizing the assessment practice smoothes the process of preparation and lessens the pressure on teachers for designing the assessment instrument (Yovanoff and Tindal 2007).

If assessment practices are less standardized, the greater is the pressure on teachers to map details of assessment. Teachers need training to design the required details for the test. Training can be difficult if administrative staff lacks specialized skills in developing techniques for administering portfolio-based alternate assessment for students with disabilities (Yovanoff and Tindal 2007; Ford, Davern, and Schnorr 2001).

The process of defining the common domains for combining student data is significant. Kentucky, the first state to use portfolio-based assessment, identified domains for all students and then selected those pertinent to students with significant disabilities (Kleinert, Kearns, and Kennedy 1997). Maryland overcame this challenge by reaching consensus on the important domains for evaluating portfolios of students with significant disabilities participating in alternate assessment (Thompson and Thurlow 2001).

There are different ways to perceive what alternative assessments look like (Ysseldyke 2003). An alternate assessment is a technique for determining the achievement of students incapable of participating in the regular state or district assessment (Thompson and Thurlow 2001). Students can participate in an accountability system by participating in normal testing without accommodations, doing regular assessment with modification, or participating in an alternate assessment. There is no single model of alternate assessment. The No Child Left Behind Act mandates states to establish appropriate alternate assessments (Alternate Assessments 2003). Presently, nearly every state has some form of alternate assessment guiding principles. However, Thompson and Thurlow suggested that most states have implemented performance-based portfolio-type alternate assessment. Teachers collect examples of student work such as worksheets, videos, electronics, photographs, and other works done on paper in the specified subject area over time and in different situations, such as in classroom with nondisabled peers (Ford, Davern, and Schnorr 2001).

Teachers date the specimens and explain the relatedness to the state's curriculum or student's grade level, and the correctness of the work, as well as the level of independence the student demonstrated. Many states use checklists or observations by teachers. Students may also be required to submit a reflective evaluation of the portfolio entries (Alternate Assessments 2003). Alternate assessment appears to be different in each state. However, the decision represents the perception of educators at the state level. Alternate assessment ought to reflect the extent to which students have acquired functional skills that can lead to some form of self-governance while having access to the general education curriculum (Ford, Davern, and Schnorr 2001, and Brynes 2004).

The Study of State and Local Implementation (2003) suggested that to comply with the No Child Left Behind Act, alternate assessment must connect to the general curriculum. Nearly 90 percent of the fifty states utilize the same content standards for students with significant disabilities and regular education students. Teachers must become familiar with individual state requirements and attempt to gain competency in each subject area and the organization and content of the curriculum in general (the Study of State and Local Implementation 2003).

Alternate assessments are significant parts of every state's assessment structure and are obliged to satisfy federal mandates outlined in Title I of the Elementary and Secondary Education Act. Title I requires that state assessments be aligned with the state challenging content and student performance standards and provide coherent information about student performance standards. The NCLB legislation of 2002 mandated that up to 2 percent of students identified as being significantly disabled can be documented as showing adequate proficient progress by participating in alternative assessment program of education (United States Department of Education 2003a).

It must be noted that states and school districts are mandated to do alternate assessments because it becomes important by administrative and legislative fiat. The 1 to 2 percent of students participating in alternate assessments may seem small; however, this number significantly affects the school and state achieving or not achieving annual yearly progress (AYP). Therefore, it is important because the state authorizes it. Several states are practicing portfolio-based assessment methods. Consequently, when the small percentages add together over all the states, the problem does affect large or substantial numbers of students and school systems. In the 2006–2007 initial implementation of the GAA, 9,387 students with significant disabilities representing grades 1 through 8 and eleven participated in the assessment (GaDOE 2007). This number is significant to affect students' overall academic performance and contributes to individual schools making AYP.

A portfolio-based assessment creates the advantage of engaging the learner to be an active participant in the process (Bowers 2005), while preparing documents for review and assessment (Willis and Davis 2002; Reis and Villaume 2002). As the use of portfolios expands, new issues and concerns arise regarding ways to efficiently incorporate portfolios to become authentic means of documenting student academic achievement for alternate assessments (Hill 2002). Major concerns, such as engaging the student participant, deciding organization and content, and method of assessment, are important factors for consideration beginning with the planning phase.

The 2001 reauthorization of the Elementary and Secondary Education Act and the No Child Left Behind (NCLB) Act mandate that all states and school systems must account for the test scores of students with disabilities. Since the passage of the laws, several states have introduced portfolio-based alternative assessments for students with significant cognitive disabilities as a means of satisfying federal, statewide, and district-wide requirements (Hill 2002; Bowers 2005). The issue of best practice in the preparation of portfolio-based alternate assessment program raises two concerns: that of (1) creating meaningful content to satisfy grade-level and state requirements and (2) matching students' abilities to content and IEP requirements.

Hughes (2006) posited that teachers are generally the persons whose skills and expertise guide appropriate decisions on the types of accommodations or modifications a student requires during instruction. It is vital that all teachers involved in the student's IEP become active participants in developing appropriate accommodations for use with students during instruction. Although the IDEA suggested that a general education teacher is present during the IEP meeting, usually, only a representative of the curriculum and instruction department shows up and not the grade-level teacher. By establishing a set method for all teachers to contribute to the IEP, this process sets the foundation for decision-making and preparation for students' participation in the required assessment (Thompson and Thurlow 2003).

Presently, there seems to be a fair amount of agreement regarding the importance of providing an education in which students with significant cognitive disabilities achieve meaningful outcomes, simultaneously experience learning as worthwhile members of a regular class, school, and community (Ford, Davern, and Schnorr 2001). There are now over two decades of examples of students whose lives have seen positive changes because of the participation in an inclusive education environment (Ford et al. 2001). However, on the contrary, Adam, Rigino, and Tatnall (2006) purported that numerous integration and remedial programs had proved inefficient and unsuccessful even when applying specialist instruction to students with significant cognitive disabilities.

Therefore, not all students in this group may experience the positive change. A successful continuation of this trend depends largely on the instructional framework implemented by states and school systems for students participating in alternate assessments based on the challenging standards required by the law (Ford et al. 2001; Antoniou and Souvignier 2007). Converse to the argument of students with significant cognitive disabilities, Zatta (2003); Browder et al. (2005); Ford, Davern, and Schnorr (2001) agreed that not all students with disabilities would achieve academic benefits from participating in alternate assessments regardless of the instructional strategies adopted.

Concerns of stakeholders include freedom from bias, practicality of alternate assessment, validity and reliability of scoring the portfolios, and the preparation of the teacher administering this form of assessment. Towels-Reeves and Kleinert (2006) posited that teacher preparation is crucial in alternate assessments, given that many teachers have yet to understand how to teach both functional and grade-level academic content. Coupled with this concern is the issue that many teachers are failing to understand the legal implications of these changes.

Stuart and Thurlow (2000) and Hughes (2006) postulated that when teachers are embarking on new programs (for example, alternate assessment), the teaching of theories with the expectation that teachers will effectively apply these theories is an unsatisfactory approach to teacher preparation. Instead, teacher preparation becomes effective when teachers understand the connection between ideas learned, how to construct practical knowledge, and make suitable application to the learning environment (Hughes 2006; Perry and Power 2004).

The problems relating to the adoption of identical standards are confusing when standards developed for the mainstream students transform into assessable benchmarks (sometimes referred to as alternate performance indicators) for students with significant disabilities. In trying to make some standards meaningful, educators opt to utilize one of two approaches: Approach A simplifies the regular standard until more suitable standard develops. Approach B redefines the mainstream standard so that it symbolizes some kind of functional skill (Ford, Davern, and Schnorr 2001).

Educational reforms place numerous challenges on administrators and teachers alike. Little (2000) shared the view that teachers play the most significant role in implementing the curriculum changes necessary to impact the students' academic progress. Turner, Baldwin, Klienert, and Kearns (2000) examined the distinctive length of time it took the teacher to assemble the portfolio and contended that the process is very demanding on the teacher's time. In support of this observation, Zatta (2003) agreed some teachers might not be willing to put forth the effort required to produce a portfolio that accurately represents the student current program. Even without much professional development and preparation, administrators and school systems expect teachers to assume and put reform proposals into practice immediately. Zatta further agued,

> The challenge of these reforms helps to facilitate teacher understanding of the underlying principles of the reform while also helps to unite those principles to the classroom experiences . . . the ambitious nature of this challenge has made the implementation of reform-based instructional practices problematic for teachers and states. (p. 42)

Kentucky and Maryland were the first two states to introduce alternate assessment. Kentucky uses the Alternate Portfolio System, while Maryland introduced the Independence Mastery Assessment Program (Thompson and Thurlow 2003). Other states have since started using portfolio-based alternate assessment. For example, Georgia introduced the Georgia Alternate Assessment in 2006–2007 school year (GaDOE 2006). Thurlow, Lazarus, Thompson, and Morse (2005) contended that over the last decade, fifty states had attempted to introduce education reforms that emphasized accountability for student academic achievement. Research done by Johnson and Arnold (2001) revealed that twenty-five of the fifty states, alternate assessment program used some type of portfolio to show proof of students' progress in relationship to the states content standards.

State organizations continue to develop as federal guidelines mandate the inclusion of more students in the assessment and accountability systems. The focus is to search for a way to assess students' achievements with recognition of the challenging academic standards while holding school districts and states responsible for results demonstrating progress (Thompson and Thurlow 2003).

Statewide assessment has become the norm for schools to account for student achievement. The results of statewide assessment provide policy makers with information for planning and decision-making to advance education curriculum and point to areas needing further research (Thurlow et al. 2005). As states focus on improving the accountability systems to advance education, one area of uneasiness is that students with disabilities might not benefit from such reform (Thurlow et al.).

Over the last decade, several states have adjusted alternate assessments to include a more intensive academic emphasis (Thompson, Thurlow, Johnstone, and Alterman 2005). Some states have also generated new curriculum frameworks and organized ways of making grade-level content available to students with significant disabilities (Kentucky Department of Education 2000; Massachusetts Department of Education 2001; South Dakota Department of Education 2001; GaDOE 2006). Recent improvement in curriculum development has become resourceful on how to plan to access the general curriculum (Hitchcock, Meyer, Rose, and Jackson 2002; Cushing, Clark, Carter, and Kennedy 2005), how to modify the academic content to incorporate students with significant disabilities participating in alternate assessment (Kleinert and Kearns 2001), and how to teach academic content to students with significant disabilities (Browder and Spooner 2006). According to Roach, Elliot, and Webb (2005), the Wisconsin Alternate Assessment (WAA) is an assessment of the academic achievement of students with significant disabilities and is different from the traditional standardized achievement tests. Like the WAA, alternate assessments are federal mandates and are required to link with state content standards.

Portfolio-Based Assessment

There is not a great amount of documentation on the use of portfolio-based assessments for students with significant cognitive disabilities. Boerum (2000) posited that portfolio-based assessment comprised a combination of quantitative and qualitative data to generate a broader reflection of learning of special education students. The value of portfolio-based assessment in communicating skills and talents and in reflecting progress is important to students' involvement in the process. The portfolio-based alternate assessment aims at measuring the achievement of students with learning disabilities. This population of students is unable to participate in the general statewide assessments.

The purpose of this form of assessment is also to satisfy state educational standards for those students with significant cognitive disabilities (IDEA; Lignugaris-Kraft and Marchand-Martella 2001). Portfolio-based assessment involves collecting multiple forms of data to support inferences about student achievement in skills or content areas that go without sampling by a direct and single measure (State and Disabilities Education Act 2003). Browder et al. (2005) contended that content validation of alternate assessment and a high correlation between the alternate assessment and the traditional assessment are significant to the process.

According to Lignugaris-Kraft and Marchand-Martella (2001), Thompson and Thurlow (2001), and Browder et al. (2003), standardized assessment tools are the least effective means of evaluating the progress of students with significant disabilities. A portfolio-based assessment makes the measurement of student progress more individualized, more truthful, and more characteristic of students' present achievement. White (2004) contrasted the contents of a portfolio to a motion picture as opposed to a particular test that is like a onetime snapshot. Portfolio-based alternate assessment facilitates students with significant cognitive disabilities to participate in a practical way, by helping to select the pieces of work that would more accurately reflect students' performance.

The states select the criteria for portfolio-based assessment in alignment with the challenging curriculum standards required by federal mandate (Skawinski and Thibodeau 2002). Contents of the portfolio, in effect, examine and validate progress and performance. The school systems support the argument that preparing work for the portfolio seems to be a more positive way of engaging students with disabilities in learning and helps develop the skills of self-reflection and self-evaluation. A meaningful collection of student's work reveals the growth, the attempts made, and the achievements (Skawinski and Thibodeau).

White (2004) contended that student portfolio is an alternative way of encouraging and evaluating all students, inclusive of those with learning disabilities. Student portfolios, otherwise referred to as learning portfolios, lean toward meeting the needs of various formats and learning outcomes, as well as for alternate assessment of students' work. Portfolio-based assessment can be used to record and complete a course, or specific parts of a course, or as an alternate way of assessing students' performance over a period.

Alternate assessments are significant parts of every state's assessment structure and are obliged to satisfy federal mandates outlined in Title I of the Elementary and Secondary Education Act. Title I requires that state assessments shall be aligned with the state challenging content and student performance standards and provide coherent information about student performance standards. The NCLB legislation of 2002 mandated that up to 1 percent of students identified as being significantly disabled may be documented as showing adequate proficient progress by participating in alternative assessment program of education (United States Department of Education 2003a).

A portfolio-based assessment creates the advantage of engaging the learner to be an active participant in the process (Bowers 2005), while preparing documents for review and assessment (Willis and Davis 2002; Reis and Villaume 2002). Teachers also recognized that the benefit of the portfolio-based assessment was associated with students' results (Klienert and Kearns 2001). As the use of portfolios expands, new issues and concerns arise regarding ways of efficiently incorporating portfolios to become authentic means of documenting student academic achievement for alternate assessments (Hill 2002).

Teacher Preparation

Because students with significant disabilities were exempted from the accountability scheme until recently, the inclusion of this population of students into the school accountability system as mandated by No Child Left Behind generates difficulties for most states and schools. Teachers of students with significant disabilities feel pressured to improve alternate assessment results without the knowledge of how to accomplish this task (Browder et al. 2005). Demonstrating adequate yearly progress (AYP) on state standards requires teachers to function beyond current research on curriculum for students with significant disabilities and to utilize instructional strategies that may not be normal practice, which is performing outside the box (Alternate Assessment 2003).

The 1983 publication of the federal report entitled *A Nation at Risk* increased public interest about the state of the American educational system. While several reforms geared at advancing the educational system resulted in the essential component of the role of the classroom teacher was missing (National Board for Professional Teaching Standards 2003). Policy makers and legislators are now recognizing that teacher-based expertise is the most significant factor impinging on student achievement (Jones 2004).

Jones also suggested that colleges and universities must change the model of teacher preparation and training to improve the quality of instruction. Feistritzer (2001) believed that "the whole fabric of teacher preparation seems to be coming unraveled" (p. 56) and teacher preparation has lost its authenticity. Dillon argued that national and state awareness of the quality of teachers, in addition to high attrition rates and the accountability structures, have amplified the demands for changes to the model of teacher preparation.

The shortage of teachers for students with disabilities results in regular staff turnover (Berger and Burnette 2001). Most newly assigned teachers may be attempting to gain proficiency at the job and at the same time confronting federal obligations to accomplish the state alternate assessment. There is a need to advance training and preparation specifically connected to the obligations of alternate assessment and to assess this training in relationship to genuine school curriculum with teachers of different levels of practice (Browder et al. 2001).

The shortage of teachers of students with significant disabilities is appropriately recorded at both state and national levels. Berger and Burnette (2001) reported that nationally, 98 percent of school districts indicate shortages in the number of qualified teachers of students with disabilities. Provisionally, certified teachers fill thousands of the special education teaching positions while several other positions are vacant according to the United States Department of Education (2000). The American Association for Employment in Education (2001) supported the research on teacher shortage by suggesting that special education teachers are in the greatest demand in the United States. Teacher shortage coupled with a high rate of attrition make the federal and state mandates more challenging for special education teachers.

The number of special education teachers available and committed to offer adequate and efficient service to the special education population raises much concern for all stakeholders. Efforts made to address the grave special education teacher shortage vary from state to state. The federal law requires teachers of students with significant disabilities to be highly qualified and have abilities to offer appropriate instruction for student academic success (Hill 2002). States and school districts adopt different methods to deal with shortage of special education teachers (Henderson, Klein, Gonzalez, and Bradley 2005). For example, findings from a survey of 983 teachers in five states practicing alternate assessments (portfolio, performance tasks, and checklists) showed that 39 percent of the teachers received conditional certification to relieve teacher shortage (Flowers et al. 2005).

Agran, Alper, and Wehmeyer (2002) indicated that most teachers question the importance of grade-level content for students with significant intellectual disabilities. In support of this view, Browder et al. (2006) agreed that alternate assessment does not promote access to the general education curriculum standards as some educators and policy makers put forward. Specialists in severe disabilities are also querying the meaningfulness of several of the skills that states and school districts are utilizing to widen the curriculum standards to the special education group of students (Ford, Davern, and Schnorr 2001).

Teacher preparation on the initiatives of education reform has significant impact on the implementation of procedures and subsequent results. Gersten, Chard, and Baker (2000) and Zatta (2003) postulated that teachers receive motivation to implement new curriculum initiatives when appropriate preparation becomes available in the form of technical assistance prior to the start of the project. Teacher level of understanding and cooperation, coupled with prior experience and skills in instructional strategies, are significant to introducing new instructional techniques and practices.

Gersten et al. (2000) also suggested that teacher's understanding and enthusiasm to think about new content and pedagogical techniques are significant to the initiation of any activity or program. Little (2000) agreed with Gersten et al. that the impact of the teacher understanding of the reform will influence initiatives and outcomes of the reform while encouraging teachers to form specific attachment to the reform initiatives. Little suggested that until teachers receive preparation and training in being efficient in adapting and transferring these skills into learning situations for students with disabilities, the effort is futile. Little further contended that, through preparation and training, the teacher transforms the curriculum into learning for all students.

Results of a study done by Kampfer, Kleinert, Kearns, and Horvath (2001) demonstrated that an association exists between instructional variables and alternate assessment results. Results of students participating in the portfolio-based alternate assessment correlated with the quality of teaching instruction received. Zatta (2003) argued that although the main purpose is for the student to have an input to gather the artifacts of alternate assessment portfolio as much as possible, it is obvious that students with significant cognitive disabilities for whom the portfolio-based assessment is most useful are limited in ability to make any meaningful contribution. Therefore, the work selected for the portfolio is most likely dependent on the experience and training that the teacher brings to the classroom. With this thought, teachers may perceive that the portfolio assessment mirrors skills, abilities, and experiences as represented in the students' performance.

Alternate assessments are increasing the expectations of most stakeholders for the students with significant disabilities to learn reading and math abilities that demonstrate state standards (Flowers, Ahlgrim-Delzell, and Browder 2005). According to Thompson and Thurlow (2001), educators in 12 percent of the states reported raised academic expectations for students with significant cognitive disabilities. In addition, 20 percent of the states reported a more rigorous education for this population of students. Nelson (2004) suggested that quite often students with significant disabilities get into the mode of achieving very little and get through with less and less because of the low expectations of educators and others. The low expectations become the self-fulfilling prophecy. Some students with significant disabilities are experiencing academic progress in state alternate assessments.

For example, in 2003, results of the Colorado alternate assessment showed that some students with significant disabilities gained the highest levels for alternate assessment in reading and math (Colorado Department of Education 2003). Massachusetts also noted a substantial increase in the number of students with disabilities achieving improved independence and accuracy in the alternate assessments results for reading and math (Massachusetts Department of Education 2003). North Carolina also documented improved results of students' academic improvement in the alternate assessment portfolio-based assessment in 2003 (North Carolina Department of Public Instruction 2003).

Writers of the assessment provisions of the 1997 amendments to the Individuals with Disabilities Education Act anticipated that the legislation would result in positive outcomes (Nelson 2004). The intention was that by requiring the participation of students with significant disabilities in state assessments, an increased participation in assessment programs would result with educators progressively assuming responsibility for academic outcomes for students with significant cognitive disabilities. Lane and Stone (2002) argued that students with significant disabilities require improved instruction in preparation for alternate assessment if this population is to benefit from the program. Therefore, teacher preparation must be part of the equation for success. Notably, most of the federal laws negated the inclusion of provision of holistic teacher preparation for this program (Nelson 2004).

Some educators and other stakeholders are against including students with disabilities in the general education academic assessment framework. States fear a narrowing of the curriculum content to include alternative assessment scores in the accountability systems (Flowers et al. 2005). Special educators do not fully comprehend or "buy into" the idea of alternate assessment. This concern needs urgent attention because teachers' interest and commitment are vital to the success of a program of this nature. Flowers et al. (2003) posited that alternate assessment generates far too much paperwork for teachers. In a study conducted on teachers' perceptions of alternate assessment (Flowers et al. 2005), it was reported that some teachers using portfolio-based alternate assessment show concerns about the administrators' nondisclosure of the number of teachers not prepared or trained to teach students with disabilities. As such, the administrators may fail to give guidance and support to the teachers administering alternate assessments because of the lack of knowledge of the process and procedures.

Flowers et al. (2006) posited that in a study of the analysis of three states' alignment between language arts and mathematics and alternate assessments, the results indicated that portfolio-based alternate assessment format is relevant to the alignment of content to standards. The study investigated how the structure of knowledge shows up using alternate assessment–portfolio-based assessment. According to Flowers et al. (2006), indications are that teachers can be successful at instructing students with disabilities if the concept of aligning content to standards is clear to the teacher during the preparation phase.

Although teachers play very significant roles, teachers are not the only persons contributing information to the IEP team. Several parents watch the children using accommodations during interactions with others such as completing domestic chores or other tasks (Thompson and Johnstone 2002). Such information becomes meaningful in deciding the most appropriate accommodations to suit the student needs although the accommodations started at home.

Thompson and Thurlow (2000) suggested that the initial IEP meeting is the most useful time to discuss this information so that the accommodations become useful during instruction and subsequently put into practice during assessment.

Browder, Spooner, Wakeman, Trela, and Baker (2006) contended that to be effective in the classroom, teachers of students with significant disabilities must become aware of teaching to state and district standards in collaboration with the federal mandates. Over the last decade, there has been renewed interest in supporting academic advancement in the regular education curriculum including the teaching of content to students with significant disabilities that connect to state standards. States require teachers to link IEPs and align instruction to state academic content standards (Ahearn 2006).

Courtade-Little and Browder (2005) further argued that teachers need to be aware of how to align academic instruction to state content standards. To establish a better understanding of the links between content and standards, teachers need to note the importance of: (a) the implication of existing federal policy, (b) the proof of academic learning, (c) the character of national and state standards, (d) the significance of starting with universal design and general education collaboration, and (e) the idea of alignment. A clear concept of these issues plus preparation will assist teachers to deliver instruction at the level required to meet students' needs (Browder et al. 2006).

Webb (2002) posited that special education teachers must develop skills and instructional strategies to satisfy state and district requirements as well as meeting students' instructional needs. The use of accommodations during instruction is an important component in organizing students for maximizing the use of accommodations during assessment.

The preparation of students for the alternate assessment encompasses many areas of teaching important to students' success. Browder et al. (2006) shared the view that for students to have complete access to the general education curriculum, students need the opportunity to acquire academic content that connects to the standards at the respective grade levels. Browder further discussed the importance of teachers' knowledge of the students' learning styles so that individualized instruction will meet each student's need during instruction and subsequently to prepare for participation in the alternate assessment.

Learning styles are simply different approaches or ways of learning. For example, the visual learner learns through seeing. These learners learn best when pictures, diagrams, and illustrations become part of the instruction. The auditory learners listen through sounds, talk through issues, listen to others, and interpret underlying meanings by listening to the tone of voice. These students learn from reading text aloud and listening to audiotapes (Desmedt and Valcke 2004). The tactile/kinesthetic learner learns from movement, touch, and doing. These learners do well with hands-on approach and like to participate with physical objects as students explore the learning environment. Students find it difficult to sit quietly for long periods and get bored from inactivity (Desmedt and Valcke 2004).

The teacher's knowledge of Gardner's multiple intelligences (MI) theory helps in the planning and delivery of instruction to appeal to the students' seven intelligences (Armstrong 2000). Gardner's MI theory proposed that people utilize at least seven relatively independent competences when learning or building a product. These intelligences include linguistic, logical/mathematical, spatial, bodily/kinesthetic, interpersonal, musical, and intrapersonal intelligences. Although these intelligences are not dependent on one another, the intelligences do not work in isolation (Armstrong). Students with significant disabilities tend to learn more when exposed to instructional approaches that appeal to all seven multiple intelligences (Armstrong). For example, a child is likely to remember to count by clapping to a rhythm while counting.

Delsher, Lenz, Bulgren, Shumaker, Davis, Grossen, and Marquis (2004) contended that the most important goal of instruction is to support the academic advancement of students with disabilities and push these students in the direction of an extended goal of successful integration in society. With this goal in mind, the teacher preparation, skills, and abilities to use instruction techniques will influence student learning (Delsher et al.). The nature of the procedure to assess student achievement plays an important part in the whole process. According to Thompson and Thurlow (2000), assessments can be quite broad based on the levels of difficulty or, on the other hand, very contracted. In general, the broader the structure, the more difficult it is to assess; and the more contracted, the easier the assessment.

It has been concluded from the findings of the research that 80 percent of students with disabilities demonstrate problems in reading acquisition especially in comprehension of the written material (Browder et al. 2006). Preparing students with disabilities for the alternate assessment demands that the teacher becomes cognizant of student learning styles—how students learn best—and instruct accordingly (Antoniou and Souvignier 2007). Appropriate teacher preparation ought to include skills and strategies to adapt instruction to the educational needs of students with significant disabilities (Browder et al. 2006).

According to Henderson (2007), teacher preparation helps teachers modify the complexity of objectives and learning materials of the general education curriculum. These adaptations assist in meeting the academic needs of student with significant cognitive disabilities for alternate assessment. This population of students requires rigorous instruction and may require extensive supports, including physical prompts, to relate, learn, and transfer or generalize information and ability to various situations (Henderson; Browder et al.).

According to Banks (2006), teacher preparation should begin at the university and continue by the employing school district as a way of increasing instructional skills within multicultural school environments. Banks further purported that teachers adapt more easily to changing classroom situations when exposed to comprehensive preparation. Colleges of education need to revisit the teacher education programs and assist students to be cognizant of the consequences of the NCLB for classroom teachers, especially teachers of students with significant cognitive disabilities (Banks).

Factors Influencing Teacher Attitudes

Janiak's (2000) defined attitude as a teacher's individual response to educational experiences combined with other influences. Attitude can be examined from a multidimensional perspective. One element in the educational reform process that is often ignored is teacher attitude. Researches revealed teacher attitude as an important component in the dynamics of educational restructuring, as this is a major factor in successful reform proposal (Janiak). Perhaps teachers with positive attitudes are more open to training or preparation. Janiak further posited that teacher attitude toward testing practices is a fair predictor of genuine testing practices employed by the teacher.

According to Culbertson and Wenfen (2004), the survey findings of 159 teachers in a small school district showed that teachers' attitude toward alternate assessment were, to some extent, influenced by the professional flexibility that allows teachers the choice of the assessment techniques preferred. Teachers tended to show positive attitude toward alternate assessments when given administrative support, enough resources, exposure to appropriate professional development, and freedom of choice of alternate techniques (Culbertson and Wenfen). In addition, teachers tend to develop negative attitude because of the large amount of paperwork required by the alternate assessment process.

The quality of professional development to which teachers are exposed directly influences the teachers' attitude toward alternate assessment. The attitude developed may be either negative or positive (Veronesi 2008). Veronesi further suggested that when teachers have positive attitude toward alternate assessment, there exists a constant evolving and continuing vision of the future of assessment coupled with the capacity to reflect on the level of the student's engagement of the task. Veronesi also suggested that exposure to appropriate professional development on alternate assessment may change the teacher's negative attitude to become positive.

Such an action is likely to build the teacher's confidence.

The general working environment of the school influences a teacher's attitude while the teacher's culture, ethnicity, and experience influence alternate assessment and working with specific groups of students within the school community (Irvine 2003). Zatta (2003) also articulated the real difficulties affecting teachers using portfolio assessment, which included the amount of time involved, the expenditure, and difficulties with planning portfolios, categorizing, and organizing the contents. These, in addition to other factors, influence the teacher's attitudes toward this type of assessment (Zatta

2003). Additionally, further investigations are necessary to examine the influence of teacher attitudes toward preparation and experience (Donovan and Cross 2002; Artiles, McLaughlin, and Pullin 2001). Teachers receiving preparation and having experience in portfolio use usually exhibit positive attitudes (Zatta).

Teacher Experience

The educational philosopher Dewey (1989) postulated that experiential education emphasizes the central role of the student as active learner in the instructional process. Dewey emphasized that teachers' experiences can be cognitive as well as physical in nature. Dewey further contended that the grounding concepts in teacher experiences conceptualizes meaning and promotes complex understanding and the desire to continue learning (Bliss and Mazur 2002).

The National Center on Educational Outcomes–Idaho (2007) suggested that while the system in each state utilizes the expertise of teachers' experiences with alternate assessment, the experience is challenged by the variability in the approach and complexity with which different students may perform the identical academic content. Castanea and DiMartino (2007) argued that some experienced teachers tend to be more open to adopting new and practical approach to alternate assessment while others give resistance to the change. Some experienced teachers claim to obtain satisfaction from getting power to design and conduct the assessments.

Castaneda and DiMartino (2007) further contended that teachers' experiences in instruction for alternate assessment have a propensity to reverse the archetypal paradigm. Experiences are gained from the opportunities to question instructional choices, to look back critically at what worked and what did not work, and to attempt to figure out why. Teachers experienced in alternate assessments usually work to establish a solid foundation and then put into practice new and varied methods of executing the assessment based on state or district's standards and guidelines (Castaneda and DiMartino).

A study conducted by Klienert et al. (1999) emphasized the necessity for additional examination concerning the degree to which teacher experience, attitude, ability, and recency effect of teacher preparation or other significant teacher attributes were related to the teacher's adaptation of teaching methods and teacher awareness of the student's gain from alternate assessment (Zatta 2003). There seems to be some indication that teachers with superior experience, capability, and preparation are prone to construct a portfolio that obtains a higher score than a teacher new to the practice of creating the alternate assessment (Zatta). Research studies of the assessment of students with significant disabilities show that special education teachers are often unfamiliar with the standards and content included on assessments (Hager and Slocum 2005).

Summary

The literature and research questions guided the study on the relationship between teacher preparation, teacher experience, and teacher attitude toward alternate assessment for students with significant cognitive disabilities. In preparing teachers to meet the demands of the federal mandates, teacher education programs must adequately prepare teachers to understand federal and state laws governing educating students with significant cognitive disabilities and to adapt differentiated instructional strategies to instruct this population of students. Teacher preparation, teacher experience, and teacher attitude must guide special education teachers toward developing a mind-set of being committed and wanting to continue working with this population of students. Much of the quality of teacher preparation depends on the value of college training, followed by the professional development provided by individual school district and teacher ability, interest, and commitment.

CHAPTER 3

Methodology

The purpose of this descriptive study was to examine the relationship between teacher preparation, teacher attitude, and administering the alternate assessment to students with cognitive disabilities. This study used a mixed-methods design. The quantitative nature of the study was derived from the outputs from the survey using a Likert scale. The qualitative framework accounted for the descriptive nature of the design, as the researcher sought to explore any relationship between the variables. The research methods described sought answers to the following research questions:

RQ1. What is the individual teacher's attitude in administering the alternate assessment?
RQ2. Is there a relationship between teacher experience and attitude in administering the alternate assessment?
RQ3. How has teacher preparation influenced the administration of alternate assessment?

Using a survey, the responses to the questions assisted in collecting data in response to questions 1 and 2, by examining any correlation between teacher attitude and how the teacher administered the alternate assessment. This allowed the researcher to obtain a quantitative perspective from the study sample with statistical relevance of the relationship between teacher attitude and administering the alternate assessment. Additionally, by using an open-ended questionnaire to examine how college preparation and state training affected how the alternate assessment was actually implemented, the responses provided answers to question 3.

Research Design

This type of research design was adequate in giving the most detailed answers based on the purpose of this research. Creswell (2003) stated that the methodology with the least variation is a quantitative methodology and is the best method used to determine how one or more variables influence an outcome. Qualitative methodologies are more exploratory and are the best means of providing answers when theory is unknown (Creswell). While the literature supports positive outcomes of teacher training/preparation and students' performance on the alternate assessment (Zatta 2003), there is a void in the literature regarding the association between teacher attitude, experience, and preparation and how the teacher administered the alternate assessment. The body of major research on alternate assessment also indicated the existing gap and the need for further study on the relationship between teacher preparation, teacher experience, and teacher attitude toward alternate assessment concerning students with significant cognitive disabilities (Browder et al. 2005 and Henderson 2007).

One of the great advantages of surveys is the vast amount of data that can become available within a short period (Patton 2002). Several respondents can respond to a survey within a few days. The average person spends a short time to respond to surveys using pen and paper. Researchers in education and other fields are finding the use of pen-and-paper surveys efficient and flexible for data collection (Patton).

Selection of participants. The demographics of "Carmel" school indicates that it is a comparatively small district with 25,062 households and a student enrollment of 11,797 with a student per teacher ratio of 14:7. Of this number, 38.9 percent of students are socially disadvantaged and receive free or reduced-price lunch. A breakdown of ethnicity revealed the following: white–73.4 percent, black–19.5 percent, Hispanic–3.0 percent, Asian / Pacific

Islander–1.6 percent, American Indian / Alaska Native–0.3 percent, Multiracial–2.2 percent (School Matters 2008). Students with disabilities account for 11.8 percent of the school population. See figure 1 for summary of demographics.

Figure 1: School District Demographics

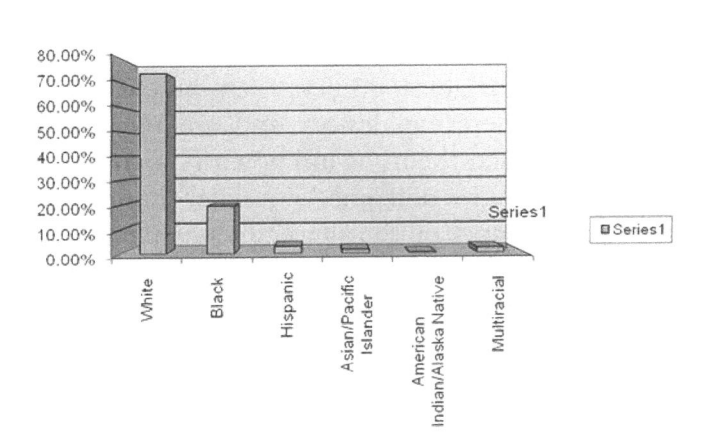

Students with disabilities total 11.8% of the school

[Bar chart showing percentages for White, Black, Hispanic, Asian/Pacific Islander, American Indian/Alaska Native, and Multiracial categories; Series1]

In terms of revenue expenditure, the district spends $8,954 per student annually. The 2006 household income distribution ranges from $14,999 to $150,000 (School Matters 2008).

The school district made annual yearly progress (AYP) in the 2006–2007 school year with a district reading proficiency score of 85.7 percent and math proficiency, 83.8 percent. Teachers with bachelor's degree represent 49.8 percent; master's degree, 40.3 percent; master's +30 hours, 9.1 percent; and doctoral degree, 0.6 percent. Teachers' average years of teaching experience is 11.5 years (School Matters 2008). There are just over 800 practicing teachers in this district. This information is summarized in figure 2.

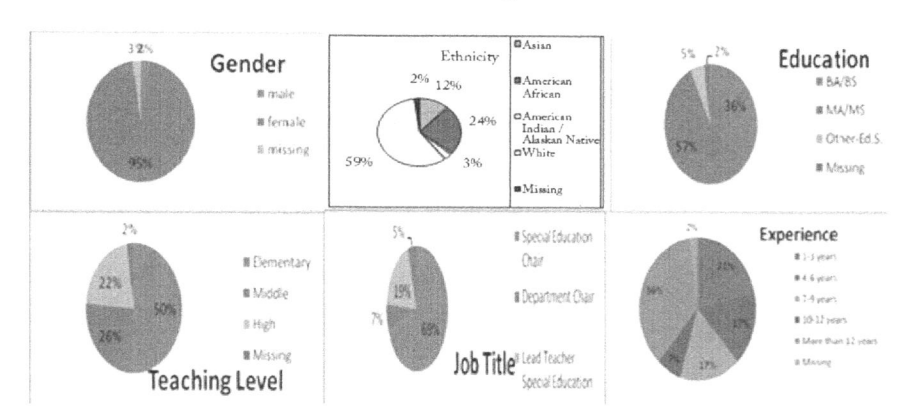

Figure 2: Demographics of Participants

The selection of participants in this study represented the convenience and opportunity sampling, considering that this is a specialized group of teachers. Patton (2002) referred to this as purposeful sampling. The study sample consisted of approximately forty-two special education teachers with experience in administering alternate assessment in one school district in Southeastern United States. Participants included special education teachers from elementary, middle school, and high school employed in one urban school district in Southeastern United States. Most of the public schools in this district offer special education program that requires teachers to administer the GAA. At the elementary level, grades K–2 assemble portfolios in English language arts and math; grades 3–5 participate in the portfolio-based alternate assessment in English language arts, math, science, and social studies. At the middle school, grades 6–8 students use this form of assessment in the four named subject areas and also grade 11 at the high school level (GaDOE 2008). The GAA is a significant element of the Georgia Student Assessment Program, which guarantees access to a challenging curriculum to all students. The state mandated these grade-level students with IEPs to participate in alternate assessment (GaDOE 2006). However, not all students with IEP participate in the alternate assessments. As required by federal mandates, only students with significant cognitive disabilities making up the 1 to 2 percent of special education students participate in alternate assessments.

Instrumentation

In an attempt to examine if a relationship exists between teacher preparation, teacher attitude, and teacher experience in administering alternate assessment to students with significant cognitive disabilities, the collection of data will be concurrent and multidimensional, involving the teachers' opinions from survey and open-ended questionnaire.

Survey. An alternate assessment teacher survey that was developed and used by Kearns, Klienert, and Towels-Reeves (2006) of the National Alternate Assessment Center, Kentucky, was used to collect quantitative data. (See appendix F for copy of survey.) This survey was utilized as the instrument to collect data from teachers because surveys are the most efficient tool for polling large samples of respondents within a short period of time. Results of research have indicated that survey helps respondents be more truthful as it provides anonymity of the self-administered instrument (Patton 2002). The survey had a scale rating from 1 to 5, with 5 being the highest rating. The survey consisted of three parts. The first section contained a cover letter and instructions for responding to the survey statements. The second section consisted of survey items. Consent forms accounted for the third section. For the purpose of this study, an abridged version of the original survey was used with the permission of Dr. Towels-Reeves, research coordinator for the center in Kentucky. (See appendix A for copy of permission to use.) A pilot study was implemented with persons other than research participants prior to administering the survey. (See appendix F for a copy of the survey.)

Open-ended questionnaire. The use of self-administered questionnaire was a suitable way of collecting data because it made it convenient for the researcher to collect data based on an individual's beliefs and perceptions. The questions specifically focused on the teachers' exposure to training and development, both in the college setting and while in service as active teachers. As a means of convenience, the questionnaire was administered at the same time as the survey. In a pencil-and-paper instrument developed by the researcher, respondents inferred to what the selected five questions mean and responded accordingly. In open-ended questionnaires, the researcher inferred what the respondents mean (Patton 2002). (See appendix G for a copy of the questionnaire.)

Pilot Study

The researcher implemented a pilot study at one middle school prior to the actual on-site data-collection visits. The pilot study was used to refine data-collection tools with respect to content validity of the questionnaire. Five special education teachers participated in the pilot study. The gender, education, and tenure of the participants in the pilot study were consistent with similar makeup of the actual study sample. Feedback solicited was concerned with the clarity of the questions and the structure of the questionnaire. This formative data from the pilot study informed the researcher that no adjustment was needed on the research tools.

Data-Collection Procedures

The participants were selected based on the roles as special education teachers employed by one school district in Southeastern Georgia. Upon approval from the Internal Review Board (IRB), the researcher submitted a letter of explanation of the study to the superintendent, principals, and educators of "Carmel" school district, soliciting permission and support for the use of the facilities to conduct this study. After receiving permission from the office of the coordinator for testing and research and principals in the school district, the researcher made detailed arrangements by phone with each principal to visit faculty meetings and distributed letter of consent (appendix E) and administered survey (appendix F) and questionnaire (appendix G) to participants. Completed surveys and questionnaires were collected by an assigned teacher in the special education department and returned to the researcher. The researcher arranged a second visit to distribute and complete the survey and questionnaire for absent participants. Participation was strictly voluntary.

Survey and open-ended questionnaire. The survey and open-ended questionnaire instrument were distributed at faculty meetings at participating schools within the district. Participants completed the survey and rated each descriptor by providing one response to each question using a five-choice Likert scale, 5 being the highest, to provide a numeric descriptive analysis based on each teacher's feedback on teacher attitude. The questionnaire consisted of thirty-six questions, which focused on teacher preparation, teacher experience, teacher attitude, and the relationship to administering the alternate assessment. The participants completed the questionnaire by responding in writing to the six questions. Respondents were asked to give detailed information in response to questions.

Assumptions

The study proceeded based on the assumptions that rules and regulations of Argosy's Institutional Review Board and/or the school district were adhered to. All procedures followed the design of the study. Teachers were asked to respond honestly to survey questions and open-ended questionnaire. Selected instruments were aligned with the topic and adequately measured the identified area of research. Further assumptions were that anonymity of participants and research sites were maintained while researcher and participants preserved high ethical and professional standards.

Data Analysis

The analysis of this study utilized both qualitative and quantitative research methods. Collection of the qualitative data focused on open-ended questions that were analyzed using content analysis and simple descriptive statistics. Analysis of the quantitative data applied the average of items meant to measure one scale or characteristic. The focus of this methodology specified the relationship among several variables. The first goal was to analyze and determine if there was a relationship between teacher attitude and administering the alternate assessment. The second goal was to explore how teacher preparation might influence the administration of the alternate assessment, and the third goal was aimed at determining the extent to which teacher preparation influenced the attitude of teachers in administering alternate assessment. The interpretive nature of qualitative research allowed the researcher to interpret the data, while quantitative procedures provided an analysis of numerical data (Creswell 2003).

Qualitative data analysis. The open-ended questionnaire was used to provide qualitative data on teacher preparation relating to activities such as college courses and professional development; and teacher experience was defined as the number of years the teacher had taught. Creswell (2003) determined that the purpose of the coding system was "to generate a description of the setting or people as well as categories for analysis" (p. 193). Once the raw data were collected from the open-ended questionnaires, responses were organized into categories in vivo (the language of the participants) and according to the guiding questions in the questionnaire.

Partial and/or complete sentences, concepts, short phrases, and key ideas that are credible, unique, and supportive in content were isolated and then grouped according to similarities (Patton 1990). A code was developed once the text data was immersed and crystallized per vivo (Creswell 2003). The five steps employed as necessary to inductively develop this code included (a) reducing raw information, (b) identifying themes based on conspicuousness, (c) comparing themes across subsamples by looking at grouped information, (d) creating a code, and (e) determining the reliability of the code by the number of times it appears from the different participants (Creswell 2003). The identified themes were represented in the qualitative narrative so that the data could be correctly interpreted.

Preliminary questions for the questionnaire. The problem that framed this descriptive study was the issue of whether there is a relationship between teacher preparation and teacher attitude toward the teachers' administering of the alternate assessment to the students with significant cognitive disabilities. Although a great deal of literature exists on alternate assessment, a gap exists for data on the relationship between teacher preparation, teacher experience, teacher attitude, and administering alternate assessment. No study so far has demonstrated any association between teacher preparation, teacher attitudes, teacher experience, and administering alternate assessment (Kampfer et al. 2001). The following research questions, along with the preliminary questions designed for the open-ended questionnaire in this study, helped determine whether there was an association between teacher experience and teacher preparation and how a teacher administered the alternate assessment.

RQ1. What is the relationship between an individual teacher's attitude in administering the alternate assessment?
RQ2. Is there a relationship between teacher experiences and attitude in administering the alternate assessment?
RQ3. How has teacher preparation influenced the administering of alternate assessment?

Quantitative data analyses. The researcher investigated relationships among the variables by the intercorrelations. The survey provided the quantitative data of teacher attitude. These data were collected from one school district participating in alternate initiatives for students with significant disabilities. Quantitative procedures focused on the measurement of facts and the determination of relationships among variables that sought to describe the influence of teacher attitude on how teachers administer the alternate assessment (Creswell). The data from RQ1 and RQ2 were analyzed by using the Statistical Package for the Social Sciences (SPSS, version 16) software. A version of multiple-regression analysis examined the relation of a dependent variable to specified independent variable (Moore 2006). Calculations of the results were done using an adaptation of the general linear model depending on the nature and quality of the data collected. Analysis of data involved categorization, coding, grouping, and regrouping data that were gathered from surveys. Findings were reported using graphs, frequency charts, percentages, and descriptions. The data from quantitative and qualitative analyses were organized and presented in the form of figures and tables additional to the narrative form of the major patterns uncovered from the qualitative aspects of the open-ended questionnaire as two raters for reliability (Patton 2002).

Validity and reliability of instrument. This study followed both a qualitative and quantitative scientific rigor. Validity of the qualitative data was based on the frequency of occurring themes in the text, accurately describing the findings. Eliminating bias was not critical in this type of methodology, as there was no judgment of truth or nontruth. Utilizing open-ended questionnaire assured representativeness in the type of information elicited during each contact. The structure of the questionnaire allowed the researcher to frame questions in such a way to ensure reasonable response to the research questions. It was not the intention to present an objective discourse with the questionnaire. The intention was to present the opinions based on personal experience of the participant to teacher preparation and experience in administering the alternate assessment.

The survey instrument originated at the University of Kentucky Alternate Assessment Research Center, University of Kentucky, in Lexington. Kearns, Kleinert, and Towels-Reeves (2006) are the original authors of this survey that was used in a major study at that institution. Feedback from the study supported content validity of the survey. The study for which the instrument was developed was comparable to this investigation, as this study sought to examine factors relating to teacher preparation and alternate assessment of students with significant cognitive disabilities. Consequently, the instrument seemed appropriate. The researcher used a small panel of people familiar with the context of this study to improve the content validity of the instrument for this study.

After this examination, items were modified to question participants' awareness of the legal framework governing alternate assessment and other pertinent elements of the study.

Summary

Chapter 3 provided an in-depth review of the methods and procedures to be utilized in a mixed-methodology design to explore the relationship between teacher preparation, teacher attitude, and teacher experience in administering alternate assessment to students with significant cognitive disabilities. The interpretive science framework that was proposed to guide the analysis of this study was based on the qualitative methodology of open-ended questionnaires that explored emergent themes and a quantitative analysis of a survey employing the Likert scale that determined the relationship between the variables of teacher preparation, teacher experience, teacher attitude, and administering alternate assessment. The collected data from the purposive sample of forty-two participants represented the analyzed findings presented in chapter 4 using figures, tables, and percentages.

CHAPTER 4

Findings

This chapter is an interpretation and presentation of the data in response to the three research questions that guided this study. Data were collected through a survey tool and an open-ended questionnaire and analyzed using the Statistical Package for the Social Science (SPSS 16.0). The decisions regarding statistical significance followed the alpha set at 0.05 as pointed out throughout the analysis.

Restatement of the Purpose

The administering of alternate assessment to students with significant disabilities is relatively new to most states and particularly to the school districts in the state of Georgia, including the district under study. Historically, Georgia is one of the most recent states to have introduced alternate assessment for students with significant cognitive disabilities in compliance with federal mandates stemming from the 2001 NCLB Act.

Pilot Study

Feedback from the pilot supported content validity as well as being an appropriate instrument to conduct the study. Before conducting this survey, the researcher implemented a pilot study to ensure suitability of the design of the survey questionnaire for the intended population. The sample consisted of four teachers from one middle school and one teacher from an elementary school different from the study site. These participants had teaching experience that ranged between one and three years for two of the participants and greater than twelve years' experience for the remaining three. The educational qualification of these five participants included one bachelor's degree, three master's degrees, and one education specialist degree. This sample was adequate, in that there was a good representation of levels of education and teaching experience. The pilot study was useful in supporting the content validity of the questionnaire. For the multiple-choice questions, all responses were valid and distributed reasonably.

Research Question 1

Research question 1 was, "What is the teacher's individual attitude in administering the alternate assessment?"

Researchers usually use linear regression to examine the relationship between two variables (Moore 2006). However, in this survey, there was no exact variable referring to "how to administer the alternate assessment." The first fifteen of the thirty-six questions in this survey related to "teacher attitude" and "how the individual teacher administers the alternate assessment." In this case, the one sample t-test was introduced to examine the relationship between teacher attitude and administering the alternate assessment.

The null hypothesis for test was that there was no relationship between teacher attitude and how the individual teacher administers the alternate assessment. For all t-tests in this study, the 0.05 significance level was used. At first, the researcher used the one sample t-test for the first fifteen multiple-choice questions, which related to teacher attitude for the entire survey sample. This method of analysis can describe the overall mean of the respondents (Moore 2006).

Table 2. The attitudes of elementary school teachers on how to administer the alternate assessment

	N	Mean	Std. Deviation	Std. Error Mean
Special education teachers have more paperwork as a result of the alternate assessment	22	1.09	.426	.091
Alternate assessment has increased special education teachers' stress level	22	1.41	.796	.170
Alternate assessment has influenced my involvement with the development of general education curriculum.	22	1.95	.950	.203
Alternate assessment has changed my views about students with disabilities.	22	2.09	.921	.196
Alternate assessment has increased my workload.	22	1.32	.646	.138
Alternate assessment has increased positive communication between general education and special education teachers.	22	1.73	.883	.188
Alternate assessment is beneficial to student's learning outcomes.	22	1.68	.839	.179
Alternate assessment has improved the instructional strategies used by special education teachers.	22	1.82	.958	.204
Teachers need to understand the federal mandates governing alternate assessment.	22	1.09	.294	.063
Alternate assessment helps special education teachers keep track of student progress.	22	1.82	.958	.204
Alternate assessment has improved the instructional strategies used by special education teachers.	22	1.82	.907	.193
Students' IEPs reflect individualized students' needs versus alternate assessment components.	22	1.23	.429	.091
Alternate assessment does not reflect students' learning outcomes.	22	2.05	.999	.213
Alternate assessment does not reflect my views about students with disabilities.	21	1.71	.845	.184
Teacher attitudes towards alternate assessment determines the quality of instruction given to students participating in alternate assessment.	22	1.50	.802	.171

The result of the table above presents the mean and standard deviations from the individual teacher's attitude response. The highest mean was 2.09, while the least mean response was 1.09 indicating that "alternate assessment has changed my views about students with disabilities" and "students' IEPs reflect individualized students' needs versus alternate assessment components," respectively.

Table 3. The attitudes of middle school teachers on how to administer the alternate assessment

	N	Mean	Std. Deviation	Std. Error Mean
Special education teachers have more paperwork as a result of the alternate assessment	11	1.00	.000[a]	.000
Alternate assessment has increased special education teachers' stress level.	11	1.09	.302	.091
Alternate assessment has influenced my involvement with the development of general education curriculum.	11	1.91	.944	.285
Alternate assessment has changed my views about students with disabilities.	11	1.91	.944	.285
Alternate assessment has increased my workload.	11	1.00	.000[a]	.000
Alternate assessment has increased positive communication between general education and special education teachers.	11	1.64	.924	.279
Alternate assessment is beneficial to student's learning outcomes.	11	1.73	.647	.195
Alternate assessment has improved the instructional strategies used by special education teachers.	11	1.45	.820	.247
Teachers need to understand the federal mandates governing alternate assessment.	11	1.27	.647	.195
Alternate assessment helps special education teachers keep track of student progress.	11	1.45	.820	.247
Alternate assessment has improved the instructional strategies used by special education teachers.	11	1.64	.809	.244
Students' IEPs reflect individualized students' needs versus alternate assessment components.	11	1.73	1.009	.304
Alternate assessment does not reflect students' learning outcomes.	11	1.64	.924	.279
Alternate assessment does not reflect my views about students with disabilities.	11	1.27	.647	.195
Teacher attitudes towards alternate assessment determines the quality of instruction given to students participating in alternate assessment.	11	1.82	.982	.296

a. t cannot be computed because the standard deviation is 0.

Both tables 3 and 4 have the same lowest mean score (1.00), while their highest mean score was 1.91 and 2.67, respectively, indicating that "alternate assessment has influenced my involvement with the development of general education curriculum" and "alternate assessment has increased positive communication between general education and special education teachers." The least mean score was in response to "special education teachers have more paperwork as a result of the alternate assessment" at both levels.

Table 4. The attitudes of high school teachers on how to administer the alternate assessment

	N	Mean	Std. Deviation	Std. Error Mean
Special education teachers have more paperwork as a result of the alternate assessment.	9	1.00	.000[a]	.000
Alternate assessment has increased special education teachers' stress level.	9	1.11	.333	.111
Alternate assessment has influenced my involvement with the development of general education curriculum.	9	1.78	.972	.324
Alternate assessment has changed my views about students with disabilities.	9	2.00	1.000	.333
Alternate assessment has increased my workload.	9	1.33	.707	.236
Alternate assessment has increased positive communication between general education and special education teachers.	9	2.67	.707	.236
Alternate assessment is beneficial to student's learning outcomes.	9	1.56	.726	.242
Alternate assessment has improved the instructional strategies used by special education teachers.	9	1.22	.441	.147
Teachers need to understand the federal mandates governing alternate assessment.	9	1.11	.333	.111
Alternate assessment helps special education teachers keep track of student progress.	9	2.00	.866	.289
Alternate assessment has improved the instructional strategies used by special education teachers.	9	1.33	.500	.167
Students' IEPs reflect individualized students' needs versus alternate assessment components.	9	1.44	.726	.242
Alternate assessment does not reflect students' learning outcomes.	9	1.78	.833	.278
Alternate assessment does not reflect my views about students with disabilities.	9	1.33	.500	.167
Teacher attitudes towards alternate assessment determines the quality of instruction given to students participating in alternate assessment.	9	1.78	.972	.324

a. t cannot be computed because the standard deviation is 0.

The researcher examined the categorical data analysis among the teachers from the three different groups: elementary school, middle school, and high school. The individual teacher from each category of school level revealed different attitude in administering the alternate assessment. These teachers agreed that teachers' attitude definitely had some relationship with the chosen instructional strategies and, hence, the administering of alternate assessment. These behaviors, more often than not, lead to changes in the way teachers administer alternate assessment (Browder 2006).

Interestingly, in response to the statement, "special education teachers have more paperwork as a result of the alternate assessment," the high school and middle school teachers had a least similar mean of 1.00, while the elementary school respondents had a mean of 1.09. However, in response to the statement "alternate assessment has changed my views about student with disabilities," the elementary teachers had a high mean of 2.09, while the middle school and high school teachers had means of 1.91 and 2.67. Findings suggest that teachers' responses on the statements identified varied at the different grade levels.

Research Question 2

Research question 2: Is there a relationship between teacher experiences and attitude in administering the alternate assessment?

To examine the relationship between teacher experience and teacher attitude and administering the alternate assessment, the researcher applied the linear regression analysis between these variables. There were fifteen questions on teacher attitude. Researcher constructed fifteen linear models to explain the relationships with teacher experience.

The information of teachers' experience in this sample is shown in table 5.

Table 5. Teaching experience and teacher attitude 1

ANOVA[b]

Model		Sum of Squares	df	Mean Square	F	Sig.
1	Regression	.001	1	.001	.015	.905[a]
	Residual	3.901	39	.100		
	Total	3.902	40			

a. Predictors: (Constant), How many years have you taught special education prior to this year?
b. Dependent Variable: Special education teachers have more paperwork as a result of the alternate assessment

Table 6. Teaching experience and teacher attitude 2

ANOVA[b]

Model		Sum of Squares	df	Mean Square	F	Sig.
1	Regression	.328	1	.328	.814	.373[a]
	Residual	15.721	39	.403		
	Total	16.049	40			

a. Predictors: (Constant), How many years have you taught special education prior to this year?
b. Dependent Variable: Alternate assessment has increased special education teachers' stress level.

Table 7. Teaching experience and teacher attitude 3

ANOVA[b]

Model		Sum of Squares	df	Mean Square	F	Sig.
1	Regression	.000	1	.000	.000	.998[a]
	Residual	34.390	39	.882		
	Total	34.390	40			

a. Predictors: (Constant), How many years have you taught special education prior to this year?
b. Dependent Variable: Alternate assessment has influenced my involvement with the development of general education curriculum.

Table 8. Teaching experience and teacher attitude 4

ANOVA[b]

Model		Sum of Squares	df	Mean Square	F	Sig.
1	Regression	.004	1	.004	.004	.949[a]
	Residual	33.899	39	.869		
	Total	33.902	40			

a. Predictors: (Constant), How many years have you taught special education prior to this year?
b. Dependent Variable: Alternate assessment has changed my views about students with disabilities.

Table 9. Teaching experience and teacher attitude 5

ANOVA[b]

Model		Sum of Squares	df	Mean Square	F	Sig.
1	Regression	.083	1	.083	.241	.626[a]
	Residual	13.478	39	.346		
	Total	13.561	40			

a. Predictors: (Constant), How many years have you taught special education prior to this year?
b. Dependent Variable: Alternate assessment has increased my workload.

Table 10. Teaching experience and teacher attitude 6

ANOVA[b]

Model		Sum of Squares	df	Mean Square	F	Sig.
1	Regression	1.990	1	1.990	2.366	.132[a]
	Residual	32.791	39	.841		
	Total	34.780	40			

a. Predictors: (Constant), How many years have you taught special education prior to this year?
b. Dependent Variable: Alternate assessment has increased positive communication between general education and special education teachers.

Table 11. Teaching experience and teacher attitude 7

ANOVA[b]

Model		Sum of Squares	df	Mean Square	F	Sig.
1	Regression	1.063	1	1.063	1.900	.176[a]
	Residual	21.815	39	.559		
	Total	22.878	40			

a. Predictors: (Constant), How many years have you taught special education prior to this year?
b. Dependent Variable: Alternate assessment is beneficial to student's learning outcomes.

Table 12. Teaching experience and teacher attitude 8

ANOVA[b]

Model		Sum of Squares	df	Mean Square	F	Sig.
1	Regression	.043	1	.043	.057	.813[a]
	Residual	29.713	39	.762		
	Total	29.756	40			

a. Predictors: (Constant), How many years have you taught special education prior to this year?
b. Dependent Variable: Alternate assessment has improved the instructional strategies used by special education teachers.

Table 13. Teaching experience and teacher attitude 9

ANOVA[b]

Model		Sum of Squares	df	Mean Square	F	Sig.
1	Regression	.137	1	.137	1.537	.223[a]
	Residual	3.473	39	.089		
	Total	3.610	40			

a. Predictors: (Constant), How many years have you taught special education prior to this year?
b. Dependent Variable: Teachers need to understand the federal mandates governing alternate assessment.

Table 14. Teaching experience and teacher attitude 10

ANOVA[b]

Model		Sum of Squares	df	Mean Square	F	Sig.
1	Regression	.005	1	.005	.006	.936[a]
	Residual	33.019	39	.847		
	Total	33.024	40			

a. Predictors: (Constant), How many years have you taught special education prior to this year?
b. Dependent Variable: Alternate assessment helps special education teachers keep track of student progress.

Table 15. Teaching experience and teacher attitude 11

ANOVA[b]

Model		Sum of Squares	df	Mean Square	F	Sig.
1	Regression	1.857	1	1.857	3.062	.088[a]
	Residual	23.655	39	.607		
	Total	25.512	40			

a. Predictors: (Constant), How many years have you taught special education prior to this year?
b. Dependent Variable: Alternate assessment has improved the instructional strategies used by special education teachers.

Table 16. Teaching experience and teacher attitude 12

ANOVA[b]

Model		Sum of Squares	df	Mean Square	F	Sig.
1	Regression	.148	1	.148	.332	.568[a]
	Residual	17.365	39	.445		
	Total	17.512	40			

a. Predictors: (Constant), How many years have you taught special education prior to this year?
b. Dependent Variable: Students' IEPs reflect individualized students' needs versus alternate assessment components.

Table 17. Teaching experience and teacher attitude 13

ANOVA[b]

Model		Sum of Squares	df	Mean Square	F	Sig.
1	Regression	.170	1	.170	.188	.667[a]
	Residual	35.439	39	.909		
	Total	35.610	40			

a. Predictors: (Constant), How many years have you taught special education prior to this year?
b. Dependent Variable: Alternate assessment does not reflect students' learning outcomes.

Table 18. Teaching experience and teacher attitude 14

ANOVA[b]

Model		Sum of Squares	df	Mean Square	F	Sig.
1	Regression	.029	1	.029	.050	.824[a]
	Residual	21.946	38	.578		
	Total	21.975	39			

a. Predictors: (Constant), How many years have you taught special education prior to this year?
b. Dependent Variable: Alternate assessment does not reflect my views about students with disabilities.

Table 19. Teaching experience and teacher attitude 15

ANOVA[b]

Model		Sum of Squares	df	Mean Square	F	Sig.
1	Regression	2.534	1	2.534	3.445	.071[a]
	Residual	28.685	39	.736		
	Total	31.220	40			

a. Predictors: (Constant), How many years have you taught special education prior to this year?
b. Dependent Variable: Teacher attitudes towards alternate assessment determines the quality of instruction given to students participating in alternate assessment.

From these tables, at the significance level of 0.05, data indicated that no linear models of (special education teachers) teaching experience with any attitude are significant.

Therefore, teacher experience cannot predict any teacher attitudes on how to administer the alternate assessment. In other words, teacher experience cannot explain the teacher attitude. Therefore, the extent of influence of teaching experience on the attitude of teachers in administering the alternate assessment is relatively low.

Thematic Extractions from Question 1 and Question 2

Theme 1: Teacher attitude played an important role in the administration of the Georgia Alternate Assessment.

Deductions from research findings indicated that teacher attitude influenced the instructional and assessment strategies practiced in the classroom. The literature supports the observation that teachers create a more productive learning environment for instruction and assessment when teachers display a positive attitude with regard to the activity at hand (Dewey 1959). Interestingly, more than half of the respondents supported this view.

Theme 2: Teacher experience is not a crucial factor.

Teacher experience is not considered an important factor as attitude when participants administered the Georgia Alternate Assessment.

This finding was indicated by more than 60 percent of respondents. This finding contradicted Dewey (1959), whose writings supported the view that teachers' experience usually maximizes benefits to instruction and learning classroom.

Research Question 3

The following is a presentation of the data collected from forty-two teachers who comprised the study sample. A six-item open-ended questionnaire was used to collect data specific to research question 3, which sought to get a response on teacher preparation to administer the alternate assessment. The grade-level composition of the study population is as presented in table 20 below.

Table 20. The composition of teacher participants at school level

Teachers from elementary school	Teachers from middle school	Teachers from high school	Total
22	11	9	42

The six questions from the open-ended questionnaire were the following:

Question 1. What is the extent of your college experience in preparing you to administer the alternate assessment?

Question 2. Please list what you consider to be the main factor(s) for preparing a teacher toward administering alternate assessment?

Question 3. What would you do differently if you were given additional training for administering alternate assessment?

Question 4. How has your educational preparation influence your experience in administering alternate assessment?

Question 5. How have opportunities for staff development provided by your school/district met your needs for administering alternate assessment?

Question 6. Approximately how many hours of training in preparation for administering alternate assessment have your department and school district conducted over the last year?

The intent of this analysis of the study sample's response was not to objectively determine right or wrong or to generalize to the entire study population. Instead, the aim was simply to present the perspective of the respondents based on the personal experiences. There was no face-to-face interaction between respondents and researcher, and as such, there was no opportunity to ask probing or clarifying questions. Respondents were directed to be as detailed as possible, using additional pages to complete the answers appropriately. This analysis will present the raw data in vivo, according to how the study participants responded to the questions. The responses were sorted per question verbatim, and then grouped according to similarities in wording, thought, and key phrases to extract the themes, and then coded and categorized (Creswell 2003).

Thematic Extractions

Theme 1: Formal education had little influence on administering the Georgia Alternate

Assessment.

Based on the categorical reduction of the responses to question 1 and question 4, it has been determined that college experience did not prepare teachers to administer the alternate assessment but, in some instances, provided tools that teachers could creatively use in teaching strategies. The respondents unanimously agreed that college courses were nonspecific to the alternate assessment. Teachers with advanced degrees and those specializing in special education felt some measure of proficiency based on evaluative tools acquired from college courses completed. The responses to question 1 covered a range of answers that fell into three key categories.

In the first category, fifteen, or 35.71 percent, of respondents, which comprised about one-third of the study sample, stated most definitively "No" or "None" to more expanded responses such as, "Coursework did not prepare us for this type of activity," "Administering the GAA was not a part of any content from college courses," "College experience does not play any major role in administering the alternate assessment," "College experience did very little in preparation to administer alternate assessment," "None really except for the broad base teaching program," "None specific to GAA," and "Some general assessment classes."

In qualifying the response that college education did not prepare graduate teachers to administer the alternate assessment, one respondent said, "Those years we did not have special education alternate assessment that is as thorough and organized as it is today." One other individual concurred, "No, I graduated in 1994. There was no alternate assessment," and a third stated, "The alternate assessment was implemented only two years ago."

Interestingly, seven, or 16.66 percent, of respondents disclosed educational levels attained to create the second category. Because there was no opportunity to probe, these resulted in some ambiguity in intent. However, as one respondent stated, "Ten years of college prepared me to cope with difficult subjects." This led the researcher to deduce that these individuals equated educational level as a measure of preparation. This was inferred in the statements of other respondents in an attempt to connect college courses as tools that allow the teacher to administer the alternate assessment in an efficient way. Such statements included the following examples: "There was one course in graduate school which taught the method of assessing special education students. It was not specific to alternate assessment." Another respondent added, "College courses such as research methods and assessment could be beneficial in administering alternate assessment."

Additionally, in question 4, respondents were required to share how educational preparation influenced the teacher's experience in administering alternate assessment.

The responses were very similar to question 1, ranging from "Not at all" to "Only in understanding the requirements of the assessments." Again, respondents linked college education as creative tools to use in administering the alternate assessment. Several participants gave supportive statements of the ability to make modifications to the syllabus and teaching strategies, which are both crucial in preparing students with significant cognitive disabilities for the alternate assessment. Such examples included the following: "Enabled me to use strategies and modifications to lower level," "Prepared teachers to assess the students and influenced how to monitor and observe progress and to adapt to different learning/teaching strategies in the classroom," and also, "Special education teachers have to be very creative in presenting and teaching the general material to students." The following statements succinctly summed up the sentiments of the study population: "Educational preparation has given ideas and resources," "to be flexible and support changes in the classroom."

Conversely, the remaining respondents did not believe that college educational preparation had any influence or "very little impact" on experience in administering the alternate assessment and attributed years of teaching as more influential on teacher's experience in administering the alternate assessment. In fact, one respondent stated, "College courses did not train for the GAA, so it did not have any impact." Another respondent shared the frustration of inadequacy, "At times I feel ill prepared to implement without a curriculum due to my lack of training." Another respondent was most clear in pointing out that "what was learned in college had a little influence in the experience used in administering the alternate assessment. Experience and years of teaching have a greater influence for me." Yet another stated, "Experience helped in teaching methods/strategies."

The third category included teachers specializing in special education but had to try to link college education with the ability to administer the alternate assessment. As one respondent stated, "One course in graduate school taught the method of assessing special education students. It was not specific to alternate assessment." One other participant stated, "While teaching in New York, I took a severe disabilities class that made teachers create documents for alternate assessment. Alternate assessment is a little different in Georgia." One teacher referred to the length of time that the GAA has been in existence, which validated the lack of teacher preparation for administering the alternate assessment from college attendance. This respondent shared, "The GAA, as it exists today, is two years old. Teachers were trained to use many types of standardized content materials to create appropriate assessments." Another concurred, "I was trained for special education paperwork, but not specifically for Georgia Alternate Assessment." The connection was made between college preparation and proficiency when one responded added, "Some of the required courses in special education helped with the alternate assessment." A mere 27.27 percent of the sample supported the effects of college experience on teachers' ability to administer the GAA.

In general, the study sample agreed that although college education did not prepare special education teachers to administer alternate assessment, it did enhance the abilities to strategize, modify, and implement regular education standards (Georgia Performance Standards) to students with significant cognitive disabilities. Others have claimed that through college education, participants knew how to administer and understand and interpret the results of the alternate assessment. One respondent stated that understanding how to find prerequisite skills for the standards have helped tremendously.

In response to attitude, two, or just 5 percent, of respondents said that teachers were more adaptive and "were taught to do what is required, whether or not there was agreement." To conclude, the attitude of most was to "follow standards." Flexibility was a constant note in many of the comments. Nine, or 21.42 percent, of the respondents claimed, "to be flexible and adaptive in classroom settings," "to adapt curriculum standards and instruct to student's level of learning," and "to student's needs." There were testimonies of being "flexible and adaptive in using instructional strategies to transfer difficult content to satisfy students' needs." Overall, these individuals felt more capable of administering the alternate assessment and "were able to understand the rules/regulations required by the state and shared ideas among grade levels at various schools in the county."

Theme 2: Differing perceived value in training.

There was no consensus on the response to question 6, which asked about the number of hours provided yearly for training specific to the alternate assessment. Responses ranged from "Approximately six hours" to "Twenty-plus hours." A few respondents stated continued support from "the people in the county" was helpful. Additional answers were "Eight hours of optional training, three hours mandatory, and two days' work sessions." Based on the wide range of responses, this researcher deducted that there was no specific number of hours for professional development for the alternate assessment in the state of Georgia. The concern arising from this finding was expressed by the respondents' answers to question 2, when asked to list the main factors for preparing teachers for administering the alternate assessment.

Just about half of the study sample unanimously said training and staff development were beneficial. Some respondents were even more specific by stating, "Training prior to beginning of assessment." Also, "Work session with feedback given throughout collection period, release time to work on or time allotted in day for collection of data, etc." Another statement that strongly expressed this sentiment was "Providing teachers with more rigorous training, exposure to teaching strategies." Some of the respondents intimated, "Providing more hands-on support for new teachers, being able to review sample portfolios, collaboration with general education teachers to understand the standards." One respondent pointed out that "training must include practical examples of what is expected of teachers."

One respondent concurred that "more professional learning opportunities related to Georgia Alternate Assessment was necessary." It was apparent that some teachers did not feel proficient in administering the test and wanted "training for the administration of the test" that is specific to the Georgia Alternate Assessment. Several respondents were very specific in the type of training favored as more collaborative. One person stated, "Sharing ideas, teamwork, time out of class to organize." Teachers wanted to be able to see sample portfolios and be trained on setting up the portfolios and said so through the following statements: "Preservice training, looking at sample portfolios," "Training to complete portfolios," and "How to prepare portfolios." This is a testament to the position of Yovanoff and Tindal (2007); and Ford, Davern, and Schnorr (2001) that when administrative staff lacked specialized skills in developing techniques for administering portfolio-based alternate assessment for students with disabilities, it posed a difficulty with training outcomes, which could result in these differing perspectives.

Question 3 asked what you would do differently if you were given additional training for administering the alternate assessment. Eight, or 19 percent, of the respondents did not answer this question, while twelve, or 28 percent, said, "Nothing, not applicable," or

"Don't know." The other twenty-two respondents, however, gave credence to the theme that present training was missing its mark. While one person remarked, "Don't know. It would depend on what was learned from the training," another stated, "Don't believe additional training would make a difference in what was done." A most profound statement that summed up the earlier discussed theme was "Nothing. This assessment does not help prepare students to be functioning citizens—nor does it assess functional skills, which teachers desperately need." This perception concurs with Zatta (2003), Browder et al. (2005), and Davern and Schnorr (2001) in agreeing that the academic benefits derived from the alternate assessment would not be equal across the board for all students with disabilities.

To support this statement, other respondents made statements in favor of students and the issue of lack of time. Several of the respondents "help student to work very well" and "expose the child to general curriculum yet look at what is functional and priority for the child." Other respondents intimated that teachers needed more time to better prepare for the students: "Take more time," "Would plan and design lesson better if there was time," "Would be better organized and the additional training would allow me to focus better," "Would be better prepared," and "Hence, be more prepared for the stress."

The last statement about stress seemed inherent in some of the additional responses. In response to the question about what would be done differently with training, responses included the following: "Nothing, would listen to other people's suggestions/ideas," "Would take extra content area courses," "Have ideas of variety of activities," "Acquire new information—clarity," "Create better portfolios," "Organize in-depth reading of manual," and "Develop strategies for modification." These were suggestive responses that were more in line with solutions. In defense of the students, the suggestions for improvement in the assessments included "Would prefer the evaluation to be done on the ability and knowledge of a particular child" and also "Document, and gather/record evidence earlier and not waiting so late to put the portfolios together and focus on collecting data and assessment during the year." These statements appear to support the belief that teachers equate the portfolio assessments as a reflection of the teacher's skills, abilities, and experiences as represented in the students' performance (Tindal 2005).

Conversely, question 4 elicited some opposing opinions regarding the adequacy of staff development provided by the school/district to meet teachers' needs of administering the alternate assessment. There were favorable and enthusiastic remarks from nine respondents. Two respondents said, "Greatly, all the training programs were excellent" and "provided great opportunities and staff development." Others stated, "There was adequate training," "The county did a great job," "Excellent provision of time and support," "Teachers learned how to administer the GAA through preservice meetings and on-going sessions," "It helped to answer important questions concerning GAA," and also, "It met some teachers' needs for administering alternate assessment." In support of established collaboration, three respondents stated, "Being able to work with other teachers has helped tons," and "By working with other staff members who work with students with disabilities, we brainstorm ideas and get things done effectively." "Administrators have allowed for training and collaboration with other teachers."

Theme 3: Unfamiliarity with curriculum and Georgia Alternate Assessment.

Based on the conflicting opinions regarding the adequacy of professional development toward administering the alternate assessment, it appeared that a significant thread of response throughout most of the interview questions reflect the teacher's belief that the standards, curriculum, and the alternate assessment were not cohesive in ensuring the students' functional development and progress. Responses to both questions 2 and 3 provided the supporting data. Question 2 required the respondents to list what was considered the main factors for preparing a teacher toward administering alternate assessment, while question 3 asked what individual teachers would do differently if given additional training for administering alternate assessment.

Varied responses to question 2 highlighted some teachers' confusion by the requirements of the GAA. These concerns fell in two distinct categories. Twenty-two respondents (52 percent) expressed concern about the curriculum and content area and the desire to be trained on adapting the curriculum to individual students. One teacher definitively stated that "teachers needed to be updated with changing rules and regulations, and teachers need to be given ideas on ways to administer alternate assessment. It was expressed that "knowledge of the curriculum . . . is a vital component," understanding the necessity for administering such assessments and its correlation," Others inferred the need for "understanding of standards and transferring content to students," "knowing grade-level standards, goals, and objectives," and "content knowledge, exposure to strategies to break down content to student's grade level for learning to take place." This is of paramount concern because with the expectations of the NCLB and for teachers to enable the cognitive development of children with special needs to meet or exceed the standards laid down by the GAA, at the very least; teachers should be knowledgeable about the curriculum and standards being taught in the classroom. As one respondent so profoundly summed up this thought, it is so important to "be aware of Georgia Performance Standards and the grade in which teachers are teaching."

Several respondents stated that the training provided by the Georgia State Department of Education on alternate assessment was very useful. The training provided information on how to administer and prepare the alternate assessment, strategies for presenting, and information on the required procedures. Feedback, time, and support were received from trained administrators of Georgia Alternate Assessment. One respondent stated that the training "brought an awareness of evaluating students with significant learning disabilities." Others became "aware of content of curriculum and to be able to adapt to different methods of instructions." Another stated, "There were two sessions, and most of that time was spent designing tasks that aligned with standards to create a bank for everyone in the county to pull from." In addition, as concluded by one respondent, which is an important outcome to any training, "the opportunities helped teachers to do the job that is required for the school district."

In response to question 3, which asked what teachers would do differently if given additional training for administering alternate assessment, a few respondents opined, "Nothing. It is more about using the time necessary to complete assessment."

Another respondent did not find the training valuable and determined that it "did not meet needs." Yet another gave greater credit to the website over face-to-face training and said, "The staff development was useless. I followed the instructions on the state's website."

To conclude, one respondent did not believe enough time was allotted, resulting in aborted benefits. This individual said, "Needs were not fully met 60 percent. Staff development was too short and not given in-depth."

Along with understanding what the GAA is requiring of teachers, about 48 percent of the study sample expressed concern for students. Based on the comments, several teachers did not believe the outcomes of the alternate assessment were student focused. These teachers perceived students with significant cognitive disabilities were at a disadvantage in "this apparent whirlwind of confusion." One respondent listed the key factors of (1) clear understanding of the standards to simplify content to meet students' needs and (2) being flexible to using different instructional strategies for students with significant disabilities. Teachers are requiring "help to develop instructional strategies and how to teach GPS to student with significant disabilities." Additionally, there was a request for "clear understanding of the types of tasks that meet the standards and are relevant to the child;" "training in modifying content relevant to students' needs;" and "creating worksheets and projects that relate to standards and elements."

In determining the main factors for preparing teachers to administer the alternate assessment, another respondent made the profound statement of "Knowledge of student's abilities to match with the correct alternate level of assessment. Another important factor in preparing to administer alternate assessment is being able to understanding the results after the test is graded." The second part of this statement raises a red flag. If teachers are unable to interpret the results of the assessment, then the information will be meaningless and will not be useful in targeting students' needs and progress. Five, or 11.9 percent, of the respondents opined that "familiarity with students, good grasp of GPS, and prerequisite skills" were important factors in preparing teachers to administer alternate assessment. Another respondent offered that knowing the student's IEP evaluation along with the student's administered daily work was an important factor. Another respondent said, "Need more examples in aligning GPS standards." The same individual concluded, "Hard to determine!"

The researcher perceived this as a need for help, indicating disconnect and a definite necessity for specific training that is possible through professional development. As Hughes (2006) posited, the lack of preparation of teachers to implement alternate assessment in compliance with the mandates of IDEA creates new challenges in accounting for the academic progress of students with significant cognitive disabilities. There was a repeated statement of request to be trained on "how to modify the material to meet the student's level," "how to teach curriculum content to students with significant cognitive disabilities," "to adapt curriculum to the student's ability levels and to collate prescribed portfolios," "to be able to use individuality and students' needs and skills," and to "change from independent living curriculum to standardized curriculum." One respondent stated, "The GAA does not target student's goals." Another respondent also inferred that "perhaps the alternate assessment helped each teacher to take a standard that is above a student's understanding and create an activity that is relevant and attainable for the student and yet meets the standard." Yet another questioned the reasoning for administering GAA to students with significant cognitive disabilities. This suggests an exercise in futility and the need for changes in a system that influences the lives of teachers, students, families, and communities. In addition, this speaks to the need for colleges, universities, and school systems to revamp teacher preparation programs to enable teachers to adequately cope with instructional and assessment challenges (Zatta 2003).

Conclusion

In chapter 4, the researcher reported the results of the statistical and descriptive analyses of all the research questions with the data collected using one-sample t-test, ANOVA, and linear regression analysis. Findings demonstrated that there is a relationship between teacher attitude and the administration of alternate assessment. Besides, teaching preparation for administering alternate assessment is usually accomplished through in-service training rather than through college experience/courses. Further findings revealed that staff development definitely provided superior preparation. The themes that emerged from the qualitative analysis included the following: (1) formal education having little influence on administration of GAA, (2) differing perceived value in training, and (3) unfamiliarity with curriculum and GAA. Results reflect an in-depth and interesting perspective of respondents' views on preparation for participation in administering the GAA and indicate an overall concurrence with findings of the study.

Chapter 5provides an overall summary of chapters 1, 2, 3, and 4, along with implications for educational practices presented. The researcher proposed several recommendations for future implementation of staff development for special education teachers administering alternate assessment and for possible extension of the study.

CHAPTER 5

Study, Summary, and Recommendations

Chapter 1 provided the purpose and significance of the study, where a detailed exposition of the problem and background of the problem were included. The research questions and hypotheses and definition of terms germane to the study, in addition to the limitation and delimitations of the study, were established. Chapter 2 presented an exhaustive review of the literature, with supporting laws and mandates, and the findings of past studies as related to the topic. Chapter 3 was an overview of the research methodology, including descriptions of the study design, population, and procedures. Chapter 4 presented a summary of the findings based on the analysis of the data. In chapter 5, a summary of the study, conclusion, implications of the research, and recommendations for future research will be discussed.

The primary purpose of this descriptive study was to examine the relationship between teacher preparation, teacher experience, teacher attitude, and administering alternate assessment to students with significant cognitive disabilities. The researcher sought to examine how teacher preparation, teacher experience, and teacher attitude influenced the administering of alternate assessment. The outcome measures of specific interest were limited to the participants' perspective on the impact of college training and postcollege professional development, on the teacher's ability to effectively administer the alternate assessment.

This study employed a mixed-methods design, utilizing a survey instrument and a six-question open-ended questionnaire to gather data, after assessing formative data from a pilot test enabled relevant adjustments to the research tools. The data were analyzed utilizing both qualitative content analysis and simple descriptive statistics of the quantitative research methods. A purposive sampling of forty-two special education teachers from elementary, middle school, and high school from the "Carmel" school district comprised the study sample. Students with disabilities account for 11.8 percent of this school population, with just over eight hundred practicing teachers (School Matters 2008). Teachers' level of education ranged from bachelor's degree to graduate degree, with tenure between one and twelve years.

The theoretical framework for this study was based on the works of Bruner (1997), whose theory on conceptual change suggested that teacher preparation becomes more meaningful when the theory and application are combined. Gardner's (1993) theory on multiple intelligences (MI) uniquely proposed the exposure to the kinesthetic, visual arts, and domestic activities to stimulate cognitive development. Dewey's (1959) theory on experiential education contended that teaching and learning are uninterrupted processes of experience. Banks' (2006) theory that posited successful teacher preparation includes teachers' understanding of laws governing education, ethnicity, cultural diversity, and acceptance of all students regardless of disabilities.

Yet with the passage of No Child Left Behind (NCLB 2002) and the 1997 Individuals with Disabilities Education Act (IDEA), teachers have been challenged with the beginning of this high-stakes accountability movement, with the equal access to education granted to all students under the legal parameters of the IDEA. This has brought pressure on teachers to demonstrate proficiency in instructing and assessing all students, inclusive of students qualifying for alternate assessments (Browder, Davis, and Karovenen 2005). Students with significant cognitive disabilities compounded these challenges (Jones 2004), needing an alternate assessment tool that would measure students' performance equitably through mandated standard-driven education (IDEA 2001).

Additionally, there is a high attrition rate of teachers for students with disabilities, resulting in newly assigned teachers and provisionally certified teachers struggling to demonstrate proficiency in administering the alternate assessment (Berger and Burnette 2001). These challenges can certainly influence one's attitude to the task of administering alternate assessment. Based on the findings in this study, it was established that there was a relationship between teacher attitude and the chosen instructional strategies for the administering of the alternate assessment. There was unanimous agreement among teachers across grade levels on this finding. A review of the literature supports the notion that teacher attitude is integral to the educational reform process (Janiak 2000) and teacher attitude influences the individual's professional flexibility (Culbertson and Wenfen 2004).

Findings concurred with the literature, which proposed that the quality of professional development directly influenced teacher attitude toward alternate assessment, in a negative or positive manner (Veronesi 2008). Most of the participants in this study were convinced that training / professional development was an effective way to prepare teachers for administering the alternate assessment. It may then be deducted that this belief also did influence the teacher attitude negatively or positively. However, despite the findings in this study, most of the respondents indicated that more training would not be helpful. This researcher concludes that disconnect between the present training and the practical application has led to this response by the study sample.

The findings related to educational preparation in administering the alternate assessment also concurred with the literature review. The literature established that lack of teacher preparation for instructing students with significant cognitive disabilities at grade-level academic content standards and administering alternate assessments prevent student academic progress. In fact, findings of this study supported the results of Zatta's (2003) research, which indicated that many teachers became conversant about the states' curriculum only from the administering of alternate assessment rather than before.

In conclusion, the teachers surveyed signified that college experience was not helpful in preparing for administering alternate assessment. Further indication was that training and staff development were successful ways for preparing teachers. Overall, 54.54 percent of respondents did not think that college courses offered any help in regard to preparation for administering this form of assessment. Of the middle school group, only one of the eleven, or 26 percent, of the sample thought that one college course helped prepare this individual for administering the alternate assessment. All other participants thought that none of the college experience was helpful. All teachers from high schools thought college experience was not helpful in preparing for administering the alternate assessment. This finding was in direct relationship with the notion that college and university departments of education need a new approach to training that empowers teachers to satisfy federal mandates in a dynamic educational environment.

Most teachers revealed that the college education received did not help in the preparation for administering the alternate assessment.

This is a very critical finding, in that when a teacher is given a class on the premise that as a college trained teacher, the individual is prepared to manage classroom responsibilities, the unprepared teacher may feel overwhelmed to satisfy the standards for meeting NCLB mandates, and unless the school environment is aware and supportive, the teacher can develop a negative attitude toward administering the alternate assessment. From the reports of the participants, this lack of preparation has translated into the frustration of not knowing how to adapt an independent living curriculum into a grade-level content curriculum (Browder et al. 2005).

Irvine (2003) supports the notion that general working environment of the school influences a teacher's attitude and teachers receiving adequate preparation and having experience usually exhibit positive attitudes (Zatta 2003). Owing to lack of knowledge of process and procedures, administrators may find themselves ill prepared to give guidance and support to teacher not adequately trained to teach students with disabilities.

Additionally, 42.86 percent of teachers supported postcollege training as an effective way to prepare teachers for administering the alternate assessment. Other suggestions included staff development, as 47.61 percent of respondents believed staff development to be useful in administering alternate assessment. The same 47.61 percent of participants also thought that an environment for sharing ideas with other teachers, collaborating with others/administrators, getting information, and being trained in time management would be avenues for staff development to meet the required needs for administering alternate assessment. A majority of the participants (67 percent) indicated that nothing would be done differently to prepare, as participants felt very satisfied with students' outcomes. Only 8 percent of the respondents indicated the need for more preparation through advance planning, although these individuals admitted to gaining much of the increased knowledge by interacting with students.

Conclusion

The analysis for this study incorporated the use of one-sample t-test, ANOVA, and linear regression analysis to determine if there was any relationship between the variables. The three research questions that guided the study were the following:

1. Is there a relationship between teacher attitude and how the individual teacher administers the alternate assessment?
2. To what extent does teacher experience influence the attitude of teachers in administering the alternate assessment?
3. How has teacher preparation influenced the administering of alternate assessment?

Based on the results of the statistical analysis of all data, the researcher has drawn the following conclusions in relation to responding to the three research questions and corresponding hypotheses.

Research Question 1.

Based on the results of the one sample t-test question, it was determined conclusively at a 0.05 confidence level, there was a relationship between teacher attitude and how the individual teacher administers the alternate assessment, thereby rejecting the null hypothesis. The consensus of the participants was that teacher attitude did influence the chosen instructional strategies and, consequently, the administering of alternate assessment. This was also true of teachers in elementary school, middle school, and high school.

Research Question 2

Linear regression analysis was used to determine whether there was a relationship between the variables of preparation and attitude. This finding, however, was not conclusive to experience, as in some cases there was no direct influence. The evidence suggests little or no connection between prior experience and teacher attitude in administering the GAA. The experience gained from the process would benefit teachers in the long run. Based on the overall results of the survey, it is concluded that there is no relationship between teacher experience and teacher attitude and the administering of alternate assessment.

Finally, teacher experience can predict some aspects of teacher attitude and administering alternate assessment, but it does not work in most situations. Survey results further indicated that there was a relationship between teacher experience and teacher attitude and administering alternate assessment, but not necessarily with teacher preparation.

Research Question 3

The responses to this question were elicited through the use of open-ended questionnaire composed of six targeted questions. Based on the participants' candid responses, it is concluded that the majority of teachers across the board agreed that college experience was not beneficial in preparing teachers to administer the alternative assessment. Nearly 43 percent of the teachers surveyed were supportive of training over other means as the most effective avenue of preparing teachers to administer the alternate assessment. Sixty-seven percent of the teachers polled did not believe anything would be done differently if given additional training for administering the alternate assessment.

Findings showed that thirty-one, or 68.75 percent, which represented the majority of the participants, felt that college education had not given teachers the tools utilized in administering the alternate assessment. On the other hand, eleven of those surveyed mentioned that college education assisted through enhanced competencies such as presentation skills, adapting lesson plans, and implementing teaching strategies. This population received an average of fifteen hours of training yearly in preparation for the alternate assessment. Nearly half of the sample agreed that a collaborative environment where teachers can share best practices in administering the alternate assessment would be most effective and useful in staff development.

In summary, it seems that not only one variable but an amalgamation of variables is essential to guarantee that teachers are equipped to effectively administer alternate assessment. Also, to maximize the benefits to this specific population of students, in addition to satisfying intended federal mandates and meeting teachers' professional requirements, a multidimensional approach is recommended. Endeavors to provide teachers with training and necessary resources to administer GAA may be significant to foster the positive attitude needed for the benefit of all stakeholders.

Implications for Practice

The results of this study infer the following practical application for educators.

1. The data suggested creating collaborative and continuous opportunities for teachers of children with significant cognitive development to share best practices in administering the alternate assessment.
2. The perception of value in service training is very low. The data suggests revamping the structure of current professional development to include case studies and small group work to practice different strategies.
3. Since more tenured teachers tend to apply creative strategies in administering the alternate assessment, setting up mentorship for newly assigned teachers to children with severe cognitive

development could prove to be beneficial in preventing burnout and high turnover.
4. Alternate assessment has become an integral part of state and school assessment, and colleges of education can now work toward offering courses to prepare special education teachers to administering alternate assessment to this specific population of students.
5. In spite of some teachers having advanced degrees and being able to draw on skills gained from college courses, a significant percentage of the study participants felt lacking, overwhelmed, and challenged due to lack of clarity and proficiency in both meeting the needs of students and meeting the standards of the Georgia Alternate Assessment. Revamping training to include teacher input on content, length of time, and using different modes of training to meet different learning styles would be beneficial.

Implications for Research

1. Future research examining school administrators' support for first and second year special education teachers administering alternate assessment may provide interesting and valid data.
2. Future study could examine teacher's perception of alternate assessment (portfolio-based) at the elementary, middle school, and high school levels. Comparison of similar studies within similar demographics could be beneficial to educators/teacher educators in adjusting programs of training / professional development to maximize effective use of resources.

Recommendations

1. The participants appeared not to have much confidence in training given for professional development. It was also the only question where some of the teachers did not respond. Repeating this study using a more qualitative design with in-depth face-to-face interviews would allow the research to

probe and draw out some of the underlying impressions and experiences, which contribute to these preliminary responses.
2. Future study on teachers' perception of alternate assessment in relationship to students with significant cognitive disabilities is recommended.

REFERENCES

Agran, M., S. Alper, and M. L. Wehymer. 2002. "Access to the General Curriculum for Students with Significant Disabilities: What It Means to Teachers." *Education and Training in Mental Retardation and Developmental Disabilities* 37:123–133.

Ahearn, B. 2006. "Alternate Assessment." Retrieved December 29, 2007, from University of Minnesota, National Center on Educational Outcomes from http://www.coled.umn.edu/nceo.

Alternate Assessments. 2003. Retrieved June 23, 2007, from University of Minnesota, National Center on Educational Outcomes from http://www.coled.umn.edu/nceo.

American Association for Employment in Education. 2001. *Educator Supply and Demand in the United States, 1999 Research Report.* Columbus, OH: Author.

Annual Report to Congress. 2007. "Alternate Assessment." Retrieved March 2008. http://www.naacpartners.org/productsaspx.

Antoniou, K., and F. Souvignier. 2007. "Strategy Instruction in Reading Comprehension: An Intervention Study for Students with Learning Disabilities." *Learning Disabilities: A Contemporary Journal* 5, no. 1:41–57.

Armstrong, T. 2000. *Multiple Intelligences in the Classroom.* 2nd ed. VA: Association for Supervision and Curriculum Development.

Banks, J. A. 2006. *Cultural Diversity and Education: Foundations, Curriculum, and Teaching.* Boston: Pearson Education Inc.

Bergert, S. and J. Burnette. 2001. *Educating Exceptional Children: A Statistical Profile.* Arlington, VA: ERIC Clearinghouse on Disabilities and Gifted Education. EC 308407.

Bliss, T., and J. Mazur. 2002. *K–12 Teachers in the Midst of Reform*. NJ: Prentice-Hall.

Boerum, L. 2000. "Developing Portfolios with Learning Disabled Students." *Reading and Writing Quarterly* 19, no. 3:211–238.

Bowers, S. 2005. "The Portfolio Process: Questions for Implementation and Practice." *College Students Journal* 39, no. 4:754–758.

British Columbia Ministry of Education. 2005. Retrieved February 27, 2008. http://www.bced.gov.bc.ca.

Browder, D. M., S. Y. Wakeman, C. Flowers, R. Rickelman, D. Pugalee, and M. Karvonen. 2007. "Creating Access to the General Curriculum with Links to Grade-Level Content for Students with Significant Cognitive Disabilities: An Explication of the Concept." *Journal of Special Education* 4, no. 1:2–16.

Browder, D. M., S. Y. Wakeman, and C. Flowers. 2006. "Assessment of Progress in the General Curriculum for Students with Disabilities." *Theory into Practice* 45, no.3:249–259.

Browder, D. M., F. Spooner, S. Y. Wakeman, K. Trela, and J Baker. 2006. "Aligning Instruction with Academic Content Standards: Finding the Link." *Research and Practice for Persons with Severe Disabilities* 31, no. 4:309–321.

Browder, D. M., S. Thompson, K. Thurlow, and B. Jimenez. 2006. *Increasing Participation of Middle School Students with Severe Disabilities in Reading of Grade Appropriate Literature*. Manuscript in Preparation.

Browder, D. M., M. Karvonen, K. Fallin, and G. Courtade-Little. 2005. "The Impact of Teacher Training on State Alternate Assessment Scores." *Exceptional Children* 71, no. 3:67–82.

Browder, D. M., F. Spooner, L. Ahlgrim-Delzell, C. Flowers, R. Algozzine, and M. Karvonen. 2004. "A Content Analysis of the Curricular Philosophies Reflected in States' Alternate Assessments." *Research and Practice for Persons with Severe Disabilities* 28:105–181.

Browder, D. M., F. Spooner, R. Algozzine, L. Ahlgrim-Delzell, C. Flowers, and M. Karvonen. 2003. "What We Know and Need to Know About Alternate Assessment." *Exceptional Children* 70, no. 5:45–61.

Bruner, J. 1997. *The Process of Education*. MA: Harvard University.

Brynes, M. 2004. "Alternate Assessments: Frequently Asked Questions. Teaching." *Exceptional Children* 36, no. 6:58–63.

Castaneda, T., and J. DiMartino. 2007. "Assessing Applied Skills." *Educational Leadership* 64, no. 7:38–42.

Center for Policy Research. 1996. "Consortium for Policy Research in Education." Retrieved March 23, 2008. http://cpre.wcenw.org/publications/allocaions.php_.

Colorado Department of Education. 2003. "Alternate Assessment Collaborative EAG Development Process." Retrieved March, 2008. http://www.cde.state.co.us/cdesped/downloadpdfEAGAlignmentprocessFlowChart.pdf_.

Courtade-Little, G. and D. Browder. 2005. "The Impact of Teacher Training on State Alternate Assessment Scores." *Exceptional Children* 71:267–282.

Creswell, J. W. 2003. *Research Design: Qualitative, Quantitative, and Mixed Methods Approach.* 2nd ed. CA: SAGE.

Culbertson, L. D., and Y. Wenfren. 2004. "Alternate Assessment: Teacher Attitude and Practices." Retrieved January 17, 2008. http:/www.eric.edgov/ERICWebPortal/custom/portlets/recordDetails/detailmini.js p?nfp.

Cushing, L., N. Clark, K. Carter, and C. Kennedy. 2005. "Effects of Peer Support Interventions on Students' Access to the General Curriculum and Social Interactions." *Research and Practice for Persons with Severe Disabilities* 30, no. 1:15–25.

Cushing, L., N. Clark, E. Carter, and H. Craig. 2005. "Access to the General Curriculum for Students with Significant Disabilities." *Exceptional Children* 38, no. 2:6–13.

Deshler, D., K. Lenz, J. Bulgren, J. Schumaker, B. Davis, B. Grossen, and J. Marquis. 2004. "Adolescents with Disabilities in High School Setting: Student Characteristics and Setting Dynamics." *Learning Disabilities: A Contemporary Journal* 2:30–48.

Desmedt, E. and M. Valcke. 2004. "Mapping the Learning Styles Jungle: An Overview of the Literature Based on Citation Analysis." *Educational Psychology* 24.

Dewey, J. 1990. *The School and Society: The Child and the Curriculum.* Chicago: University of Chicago.

Digest of Education Statistics. 2005. "Defining Special Education." Retrieved May 26, 2008. http://eric.ed.gov/ERICWebPortal/recordDetail?accno=ED483072-24k.

Donovan, M. S. and C. Cross. 2002. *Minority Students in Gifted and Special Education*. Washington, DC: National Academy.

Ebersole, M. M., and A. M. Worster. 2007. "Sense of Place in Teacher Preparation Courses: Place-Based and Standards-Based Education." *Delta Kappa Gamma Bulletin* 73, no. 2:19–24.

Educate America Act-Pl—103–27. *All Students, Including Students with Disabilities*. Goals 2000.

Elliot, J. L., R. N. Erickson, M. L. Thurlow. 2000. *Educating One and All*. VA: Council of Exceptional Children.

English, F. W., and B. E. Steffy. 2004. *Deep Curriculum Alignment: Creating a Level Playing Field for All Children on High-Stakes Tests of Educational Accountability*. Lanham, MD: Scarecrow.

Farrington, K. 2003. "Paraprofessionals: Critical Team Members in Our Special Education Programs." *Exceptional Children* 75, no. 4:200–204.

Feistritzer, E. and D. Chester. 2001. *Alternative Teacher Certification: A State-by-State Analysis*. Washington, DC: National Center for Education Information. Retrieved February 2008. http://www.ncei.com2001_Alt_Teacher_Cert.htm.

Flowers, C., and D. M. Browder. 2006. "An Analysis of Three States' Alignment between Language Arts and Mathematics Standards and Alternate Assessments." *Council for Exceptional Children* 72, no. 2:201–215.

Florian, L. and D. Pullin. 2000. "Defining Difference: A Contemporary Perspective on Legal Policy Issues in Education Reform and Special Education Needs." Retrieved January 21, 2008. www.isec2000.org.uk/abstracts/papers_i/jordan_1.htm.

Flowers, C., L. Ahlgrim-Dezell, D. M. Browder, and F. Spooner. 2005. "Teachers' Perceptions of Alternate Assessments." *Research and Practice for Persons with Severe Disabilities* 30, no. 2:81–92.

˙d, A., L. Davern, and R. Schnorr. 2001. "Learners with Significant ˙isabilities." *Remedial and Special Education* 22, no. 4:214–216.

˙r, H. 1983. *Theory of Multiple Intelligences*. New York, NY: ˙ Books.

Georgia Department of Education (GaDOE). 2006. "Students with Disabilities Advocates." Retrieved June 24, 2007. http://cobbcast:cobbk12.org12m=20061212-16.

———. 2007. "Students with Disabilities Advocates." Retrieved June 24, 2007. http://cobbcast:cobbk12.org12m=20061212-16.

———. 2008. "Students with Disabilities Advocates." Retrieved January 28, 2008. http://cobbcast:cobbk12.org12m=20061212-16.

Gersten, R., D. Chard, and S. Baker. 2000. "Factors Enhancing Sustained Use of Research-Based Instructional Practices." *Journal of Learning Disabilities* 33, no. 5:445–457.

Goals 2000: Educate America Act, Pub. L. No.103–227 (1994). Retrieved June 23, 2007. http://www. Ed.gov/legislation/Goals2000/TheAct/USCongress,2nd Session.

Gonzalez, P., and R. Bradley. 2005. "Teachers of Children with Emotional Disturbance: A National Look at Preparation, Teaching conditions and Practices." *Behavioral Disorders* 31, no. 1:6–17.

Hager, K. D. and T. A. Slocum. 2005. "Using Alternate Assessment to Improve Educational Outcomes." *Rural Special Education Quarterly* 24, no. 1:54–59.

Henderson, K., K. Klein, P. Gonzalez, and R. Bradley. 2005. "Teachers of Children with Emotional Disturbance: A National Look at Preparation, Teaching Conditions and Practices." *Behavioral Disorders* 31, no. 1: 6–17.

Henderson, K., Klein, and D. Hill. 2002. *Electronic Portfolios: Teacher Candidate Development and Assessment.* EDRS 463261.

Henderson, S. E. 2007. *An Examination of the Content Standard Mastery of Students Participating in the 2004–2005 Maryland Alternate Assessment.* Unpublished Manuscript, University of Minnesota.

Hill, D. 2002. *Electronic Portfolio: Teacher Candidate Development and Assessment.* EDRS463261.

Hitchcock, C., A. Meyer, D. Rose, and R. Jackson. 2002. "Providing New Access to the General Curriculum: Universal Design for Learning." *Teaching Exceptional Children* 35, no. 2:8–17.

Hughes, J. A. 2006. "Bridging the Theory-Practice Divide: A Creative Approach to Effective Teacher Preparation." *Journal of Scholarship and Teaching* 6, no. 1:110–117.

Individuals with Disabilities Education Act (IDEA) of 1997, 12o USC. 140 et seq.

Irvine, J. J. 2003. *Educating Teachers for Diversity: Seeing With a Cultural Eye*. NY: Teachers College, Columbia University.

Janiak, R. (2000). "Blueprint 2000 Student Performance Standards: What Variables Correlate with Teacher Perceptions of Goal 3." *Florida Journal of Educational Research* 37, no. 1.

Janish, C., X. Liu, and A. Akrofi. 2007. "Implementing Alternate Assessment: Opportunities and Obstacles." *The Educational Forum* 71:222–230.

Jones, S. 2004. "The Implementation and Evaluation of an IDEA Inclusion Program in a Rural Middle School in Georgia." Retrieved July 10, 2007. http://proquest.umi.com.cardinal.fielding.edd/dissertations/preview_all/3158286.

Johnson, E., and N. Arnold. 2004. "Validating an Alternate Assessment." *Remedial and Special Education* 25, no. 5:266–275.

Kampfer, S. H., L. S. Horvath, and J. F. Kearns. 2001. "Teachers' Perceptions of One State's Alternate Assessment Portfolio Program: Implications for Practice and Effects of Peer Support Interventions on Students' Access to the General Curriculum and Social Interactions." *Teaching Exceptional Children* 36, no. 4:42–47.

Kleinert, H. L., P. Green, M. Hurte, J. Clayton, and C. Oetinger. 2002. "Creating and Using Meaningful Alternative Assessment." *Teaching Exceptional Children* 34, no. 4:40–47.

Kleinert, H. L., J. Kearns, and S. Kennedy.1997. "Accountability for All Students: Kentucky's Alternate Portfolio Assessment for Students with Moderate and Severe Cognitive Disabilities." *The Journal of the Association for Persons with Severe Handicaps* 22:88–101.

Lane, S., and C. A. Stone,. 2002. "Strategies for Examining the Consequences of Alternate Assessment and Accountability Programs." *Educational Measurement: Issues and Practice* 21, no. 2:23–30.

Lashley, C. 2002. "Participation of Students with Disabilities in Statewide Assessments and the General Education Curriculum. Implications for Administrative Practice." *Journal of Special Education Leadership* 15, no. 5:10–16.

Lignugaris-Kraft, B., N. Marchand-Martella, and R. Martell. 2001. "Strategies for Writing Better Goals and Short-Term Objectives or Benchmarks." *Teaching Exceptional Children* 34, no. 1:52–58.

Little, J. 2000. *Professional Development Pursuit of School Reform: Teachers Caught in the Action. Professional Development that Matters.* New York, NY: Teachers' College.

Massachusetts State Department of Education. 2000. *Guide to the Parent/Guardian Report for the 2001 MCAS Alternate Assessment*, Boston: Author.

McDonnell, L. M., M. J. McLaughlin, and P. Morison. 1997. *Educating One and All: Students with Disabilities in Standards-Based Reform.* Washington, DC: National Academy.

McLaughlin, C., and M. Rouse. 2004. *Special Education and School Reform in the United States and Britain.* New York, NY: Routledge.

Messick, S. 1996. *Validity and Washback in Language Testing.* Princeton, NJ: Educational Testing Service.

Moore, D. S. 2006. *The Basic Practice of Statistics.* 4th ed. New York: W. H. Freeman and Company.

National Board for Professional Teaching Standards. 2003. "What Teachers Are Learning." Retrieved December 28, 2007. http://www.jmt.sagepub.com/egi/content/refs/17/1/33.

National Center on Education Outcomes (NCEO). "Electronic Center for Alternate Assessment Scoring." Retrieved January 19, 2008. http://cedh.umn.edu/nceo/projects/StateProjects.html.

Nelson, T. 2004. "Special Education, Special Law." *Teacher Education Quarterly* 24, no. 4:25–28.

No Child Left Behind (NCLB) Act of 2001, Pub. I. No. 107-110, 115 Stat. 1425.

Noll, J. W. 2006. *Taking Sides: Clashing Views on Educational Issues.* Dubuque, IA: McGraw-Hill.

North Carolina Department of Public Instruction. 2002. "The North Carolina Testing Results." Raleigh, NC: Public Schools of North Carolina.

Patton, M. Q. 2002. *How to Use Qualitative Methods in Evaluation.* Newbury Park, CA: SAGE.

Perry, C. M., and B. M. Power. 2004. "Finding the Truths in Teacher Preparation Field Experiences." *Teacher Education Quarterly* 31, no.12:125–136.

Pullin, D. 1994. Learning to Work: *The Impact of Curriculum and Assessment Standards on Educational Opportunities. Harvard Educational Review* 63, no. 1:31–54.

Quenemoen, R., S. Thompson, and M. Thurlow. 2003. *Measuring Academic Achievement of Students with Significant Cognitive Disabilities: Building Understanding of Alternate Assessment Scoring Criteria.* MN. Retrieved June 20, 2007. http://education.umn.edu/NCEO/OnlinePubs/Synthesis50.html.

Reis, N., Villaume, S. 2002. "The Benefits, Tensions, and Visions of Portfolios as a Wide-Scale Assessment for Teacher Education." *Action in Teacher Education* 23, no. 4:10–17.

Roach, A. T., S. N. Elliot, and N. L. Webb. 2005. "Alignment of an Alternate with State Academic Standards: Evidence for the Content Validity of the Wisconsin Alternate Assessment." *Journal of Special Education* 38:218–231.
http://www.schoolmatters.com/schools.aspx/q/page=dl/did=6390/midx=CPTeach.

School Matters. 2008.*Walton County Public Schools Exceptional Education.* Retrieved January 20, 2008. http://Walton.k12.ga.us.

Skawinski, S., and S. Thibodeau. 2002. "A Journey into Portfolio Assessment." *Educational Forum* 67, no. 1:81–88.

Souvignier, E., and J. Mokhlesgerami. 2006. "Using Self-Regulation as a Framework for Implementing Strategy-Instruction to Foster Reading Comprehension." *Learning and Instruction* 16:57–71.

South Dakota Department of Education. 2001. "Status of Alternate Assessment." Retrieved January 24, 2008. http://nagh.org/pubs/conferences/thurlow/pdf.

Stuart, C. and D. Thurlow. 2000. "Making It Their Own: Pre-Service Teachers' Experiences, Beliefs, and Classroom Practices." *Journal of Teacher Education* 512. Study of State and local implementation and impact of the individuals with Disabilities *Education Act: Final Report on selected findings.* Retrieved June 26, 2007. http://www.abr.sliidea.org/reports.html.

Thissen, D., H. Wainer, and X. Wang. 1994. "Are Tests Comprising Both Multiple-Choice and Free-Response Items Necessarily Less Unidimensional than Multiple-Choice Tests? An Analysis of Two Tests." *Journal of Educational Measurements* 31:113–123.

Thompson, S. J., and M. Thurlow. 2001. *State Special Education Outcomes: A Report on State Activities at the Beginning of a New Decade*. Retrieved June 24, 2007. http://education.umn.edu/NCEO/OnlinePubs/2001StateReport.html.

Thompson, S. J., M. Thurlow, C. Johnstone, and J. Alterman,. 2003. *State Special Education Outcomes: Steps Forward in a Decade of Change*. Retrieved June 24, 2007. http://education.umn.edu/NCEO/OnlinePubs/2005StateReport.html.

Thompson, S. J., R. F. Quenemoen, and M. L. Thurlow. 2003. The Status of Large-Scale Assessment Practices for Students with Disabilities in Rural America. *Rural Special Quarterly* 22:3–9.

Thurlow, M. L., S.S. Lazarus, S. J. Thompson, and A. B. Morse. 2005. "State Policies on Assessment Participation and Accommodations for Students with Disabilities." *The Journal of Special Education* 38:232–240.

Thurlow, M. L., J. Elliot, and J. E. Ysseldyke. 2002. *Testing Students with Disabilities: Practical Strategies for Complying with District and State Requirements*. 2nd ed. CA: SAGE.

Tindal, G., M. McDonald, M. Todesco, A. Glasgow, P. Almond, and L. Crawford. 2003. "Alternate Assessments in Reading and Math: Development and Validation for Students with Significant Disabilities." *Exceptional Children* 24, no. 69:481–494.

Title I—Improving the Academic Achievement of the Disadvantaged: Final Rule, 68 Fed. Reg. 236. 2003. Retrieved January 24, 2007. http://www.ed.gov/policyelsec/guid/atlguidance.doc.

Towels-Reeves, E., and H. L. Kleinert. 2005. "Impact of One State's Alternate Assessment upon Instruction and IEP Development." *Rural Education Quarterly* 34:355–369.

Traub, R., and C. Fisher. 1997. "On the Equivalence of Constructed-Response amid Multiple-Choice Tests." *Applied Psychological Measurements* 1, no. 3:355–369.

Turner, M. D., H. L. Kleinert, and J. F. Kearns. 2000. "The Relation of a Statewide Alternate Assessment for Students with Severe

Disabilities to Other Measures of Instructional Effectiveness." *Journal of Special Education* 34:69–76.

US Department of Education. 2005. "Alternate Achievement Standards for Students with the Most Significant Disabilities." Washington, DC: Author. Retrieved June 24, 2007. http://www.ed.gov/policyelsec/guid/atlguidance.doc.

US Department of Education. 1995. *Individuals with Disabilities Education Act: Amendments of 1995: Reauthorization of the Individuals with Disabilities Act.* Washington, DC: Author.

———. 2003a. *Title I—Improving the Academic Achievement of the Disadvantaged: Final Rule*, 68 Fed. Reg. 236. 2002 (codified at 34C.F.R. pt.2002).

———. 2003b. *Title I—Improving the Academic Achievement of the Disadvantaged: Proposed Rule*, 68 Fed. Reg. 13,797-13, 798.

Veronesi, J. F. 2008. *Where Will Your Attitude Take You?* RN NEWS, 321

Washburn-Moses, L. 2003. "What Every Special Educator Should Know About High-Stakes Testing." *Teaching Exceptional Children* 35, no. 4:12–15.

Webb, N. L. 2002. *Alignment Study in Language Arts, Mathematics, Science, and Social Studies of State Standards and Assessments for Four States.* Washington, DC: Council of Chief State School Officers.

Wehmeyer, M. L. 2002. *Teaching Students with Mental Retardation: Providing Access to the General Curriculum.* MD: Paul H. Brookes.

White, C. 2004. *Student Portfolios: An Alternative Way of Encouraging and Evaluating Student Learning.* New Directions for Teaching and Learning, 100.

Wiener, D. 2002. *Massachusetts: One State's Approach to Setting Performance Levels for the Alternate Assessment.* (Synthesis Report: 48). Retrieved October 30, 2007. http://education.umn.edu/NCEO/OnlinePubs/Synthesis48.html.

Wigle, S. E., and D. E. Wilcox. 2010. "Fights to Include Special Education." *The Journal of At Risk Issues* 12, no. 4:14–16.

Willis, E. and M. Davies. 2002. "Promise and Practice of Professional Portfolios." *Action in Teacher Education* 23, no. 4:18–27.

Ysseldyke, J., A. Dennison, and R. Nelson. 2003. *Large-Scale Assessment and Accountability Systems: Positive Consequences for Students with*

Disabilities (Synthesis Report 51). Retrieved October 30, 2007. http://education.umn.edu/NCEO/OnlinePubs/Synthesis51.html.

Yovanoff, P., and G. Tindal. 2007. "Scaling Early Reading Alternate Assessments with Statewide Measures." *Exceptional Children* 73, no. 2:184–201.

Zatta, M. C. 2003. *Is There a Relationship between Teacher Experience and Teacher Training and Student Scores on the MCAS Alternate Assessment?* Unpublished Manuscript, Boston College.

APPENDIX A

Permission to Use Survey Tool

From: liztowles-reeves@uky.edu

To: ihard@hotmail.com

Date: Mon, 29 Oct 2007 11:50:23 -0400

Subject: RE: Request Dissertation Committee Member

Hi Icylin,

Counting down the days until "it" is over! ☺
Regarding the citation for the Alternate Assessment Impact Survey:
Kearns, J., Kleinert, H., and Towles-Reeves, E. (2006). *Alternate Assessment Impact Survey*. Lexington, Kentucky: University of Kentucky, National Alternate Assessment Center.

You have permission to use all or parts of this survey as long as NAAC (reference above) is given credit for those questions/sections.

I believe the other survey I sent you was from Lynn Ahlgrim-Delzell at UNC-Charlotte. You may email her directly to request permission to use that survey at laahlgri@uncc.edu. Please let her know you received a copy of the survey from me and what you intend to use it for. She can also provide you direct permission and a citation.

Best of luck! Sounds like you are making good progress! Liz

Elizabeth Towles-Reeves, Doctoral Candidate
Research Coordinator
National Alternate Assessment Center
1 Quality Street, Suite 722
Lexington, Kentucky 40507
Phone: 859.257.7672 X 80255
Fax: 859.323.1838
Email: liztowles-reeves@uky.edu

APPENDIX B

County Permission to Use Facilities

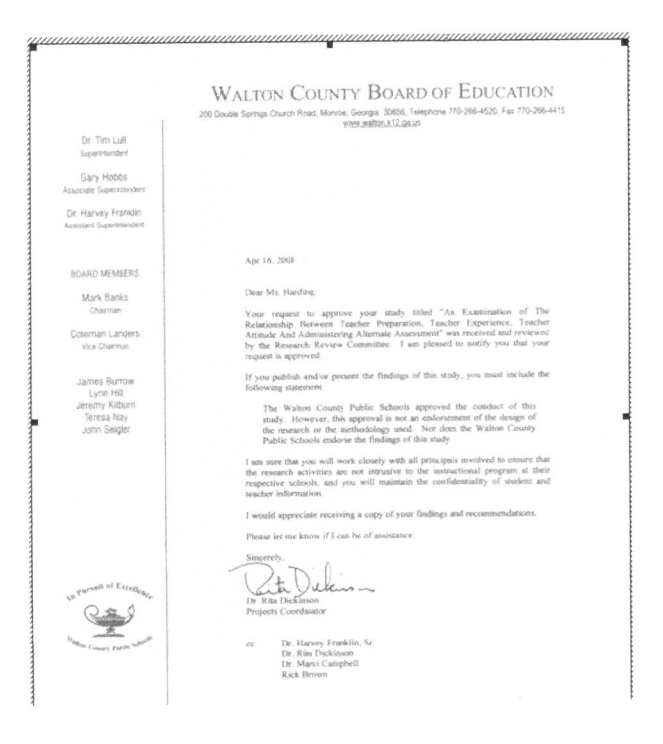

APPENDIX C

IRB Approval

MEMO

To: Icylin Harding

From: Murray Bradfield, Jr., Ph.D.

Date: April 4, 2008

RE: Human Subjects Protocol—An Examination Of The Relationship Between Teacher Preparation, Teacher Experience, Teacher Attitude, And Administering Alternate Assessment

CC: Dr. Joe Balloun

    The Institutional Review Board has **certified** your research protocol. The approval of your protocol is contingent on a letter of approval from the agency or institution in which you plan to conduct the study. <u>Before gathering any data, you must present the agency or institutional letter of approval, signed and on original letterhead, to the Argosy IRB chair</u>. The certification of your protocol is in effect for one full calendar year from the date of approval, April 4, 2008. Thereafter, continued approval is contingent upon submission of a renewal form, which must be reviewed and approved by the Institutional Review Board prior to the expiration date of the current approval, April 4, 2009. Approval is also contingent upon your agreement to abide by the American Psychological Association ethical guidelines that govern human participation in research. In addition, you are expected to comply with the protocol as presented, and keep appropriate records as to your use and maintenance of collected data.

Good luck with conducting your proposed research.

APPENDIX D

Principal Permission to Use Facilities

March 20, 2008

James Mill School
1234 Marlon Road
Loganville, Ga. 30054

Dear Dr. Luke,

In order to complete my doctoral program in Instructional Leadership at Argosy/Atlanta University, I am interested in conducting my research study at your school during April/May of the 2007/2008 school year. The focus of the study is to *examine the relationship between teacher preparation, teacher experience, teacher attitude, and administering alternate assessment to students with cognitive disabilities.*

The county office was contacted to seek approval to conduct the study at all the schools in your school district. Only Special Education teachers participating in the Georgia Alternate Assessment program are being requested to participate in this study.

Teachers will be able to read consent forms and complete the survey and questionnaire in 20–25 minutes.

With your permission, this activity can be arranged for the beginning or end of your faculty meeting.

Thank you in advance for your help and cooperation in this endeavor.

Sincerely,

Icylin Harding
Doctoral Candidate
Argosy/Atlanta

APPENDIX E

Letter of Invitation

Hello,

My name is Icylin Harding and I am a doctoral candidate at Argosy University. I am in the process of collecting information for a research study for my dissertation. I am exploring the relationship between teacher preparation, teacher experience, teacher attitude, and how the alternate assessment is administered. I need to hear from various teacher professionals who are working with children with significant cognitive disabilities. I am inviting you to be one of the participants. Your participation is voluntary, and you can withdraw at anytime. There is also no tangible incentive for participating, and the information given will be confidential. Would you be willing to participate?

Should you accept, I need for you to read, sign, and return to me when I visit your school. Once I have received your consent form, I will contact you to schedule a time to complete the survey and open-ended questionnaire. Please let me know if you have any questions. Thank you very much.

Regards,

Icylin Harding

APPENDIX F

Informed Consent for Participants Age 18 and Older

Consent Form

An Examination of the Relationship Between Teacher Preparation, Teacher Experience, Teacher Attitude, And Administering Alternate Assessment.

Dear Participant,

You are invited to participate in a research study examination of the relationship between teacher preparation, teacher experience and teacher attitude toward administering alternate assessment. You were selected as a possible participant because of your knowledge and/or experience related to the topic. Please read this form and ask any questions you may have before acting on this invitation to be in the study.

This study is being conducted by: **Icylin Harding,** a doctoral *candidate at Argosy University.*

Background Information:

The purpose of this descriptive study is to examine the relationship between teacher preparation and teacher attitude toward teachers' execution of the alternate assessment to students with significant cognitive disabilities.

Procedures:

If you agree to be in this study, you will be asked to do the following things. .

1. Complete a 30-item survey and a six question open-ended questionnaire.
2. Transcripts will be sent to the participant by e-mail, to review and verify, to make alterations, or add to as the individual sees fit. The intent is to capture accurate feelings describing your experience to educational preparation and experience in administering the Alternate assessment.
3. The transcripts will be returned to the researcher by e-mail, after which the researcher will contact the participant by telephone to discuss any changes. This follow-up call should last about half hour.
4. At the end of the study, the researcher will send by US mail a summary of the findings of this research study.

Voluntary Nature of the Study:

Your participation in this study is strictly voluntary. Your decision whether or not to participate will not affect your current or future relations with the Department of Education. If you initially decide to participate, you are still free to withdraw at any time later without affecting those relationships. *There will be no financial awards to participate in this study.*

Risks and Benefits of Being in the Study:

There is no impending risk in participating in this study.

The benefits of participation are the likelihood of enhancing the teacher development and training to address any significant findings resulting from this study.

In the event you experience stress or anxiety during your participation in the study, you may terminate your participation at any time. You may refuse to answer any questions you consider invasive or stressful.

Compensation:

There is no compensation included in this study. Your participation is strictly voluntary.

Confidentiality:

The records of this study will be kept private. In any report of this study that might be published, the researcher will not include any information that will make it possible to identify a participant. Research records and tape recordings will be kept in a locked file; only the researcher and authorized school representatives will have access to the records.

In accordance with the requirements of Argosy University, all recorded information will be retained for at least 5 years after the approval of the dissertation. Only the principal researcher will have access to these recordings.

Contacts and Questions:

The researcher conducting this study is *Icylin Harding*. The researcher's adviser is *Dr. Joseph Balloun, Ph. D. You* may ask any questions you have now. If you have questions later, you may contact them at:

Icylin Harding
Address: 3454 Midway Cove Dr. Loganville, GA. 30052
Telephone: 7705543408 (H)   6784803952 ©
e-mail address: **ihard@hotmail.com**

Dr. Joseph Balloun (CHAIR)
Address: College of Education, Argosy University/Atlanta, Two Lakeside Commons, 980
Hammond Dr., Suite 472, Atlanta GA. 30328
Telephone: 7705544308 (H)   6784803952 ©
e-mail address: jballoun@argosy.edu

The Research Participant Advocate at Argosy University is Dr. Joseph Balloun. You may contact him at (7704071128 if you have questions about your participation in this study.

Please sign and return this consent form when I visit your school. You may keep a copy of this consent form.

Statement of Consent:

I have read the above information. I have asked questions and received answers. I consent to participate in the study.

Name of Participant

Signature of Participant_____Date_____

Signature of Investigator_____Date_____

APPENDIX G

Alternate Assessment Impact Survey

For each of the statement below, indicate the extent to which you agree or disagree with the statement by circling the appropriate number.

Strongly Agree = 1 **Agree = 2** **Neutral = 3**

Disagree = 4 **Strongly Disagree = 5**

	Strongly Agree	Agree	Neutral	Disagree	Strongly Disagree
1. Special education teachers have more paperwork as a result of the alternate assessment.	0	0	0	0	0
2. Alternate assessment has increased special education teachers' stress level.	0	0	0	0	0
3. Alternate assessment has influenced my involvement with the development of general education curriculum.	0	0	0	0	0
4. Alternate assessment has changed my views about students with disabilities.	0	0	0	0	0

5. Alternate assessment has increased my workload.	0	0	0	0	0
6. Alternate assessment has increased positive communication between school district and parents.	0	0	0	0	0
7. Alternate assessment is beneficial to student's learning outcomes.	0	0	0	0	0
8. Alternate assessment has improved the instructional strategies used by special education teachers.	0	0	0	0	0
9. Teachers must understand the federal mandates governing alternate assessment.	0	0	0	0	0
10. Alternate assessment has changed my views about students with disabilities.	0	0	0	0	0
11. Alternate assessment has not improved the instructional strategies used by special education teachers.	0	0	0	0	0
12. Students' IEPs reflect individualized students' needs versus alternate assessment components.	0	0	0	0	0
13. Alternate assessment is beneficial to students' learning outcomes.	0	0	0	0	0
14. Alternate assessment has changed my views about students with disabilities.	0	0	0	0	0
15. Teacher preparation determines the quality of instruction given to students participating in alternate assessment.	0	0	0	0	0

Teacher Experience

16. Alternate assessment has changed my views about students with disabilities.	0	0	0	0	0
17. Alternate assessment has increased my work load.	0	0	0	0	0

18. Level of training influences teacher's method of administering alternate assessment.	0	0	0	0	0
19. Experience influences the method used to administer alternate assessment.	0	0	0	0	0
20. Experience does not influence the method used to administer alternate assessment.	0	0	0	0	0
21. Additional training in content/standards would benefit teachers administering alternate assessment.	0	0	0	0	0
22. Experience in pre-service preparation influences the teacher's ability to administer alternate assessment.	0	0	0	0	0
23. Special education teachers leave the classroom because of lack of experience to administering alternate assessment	0	0	0	0	0
24. Training prior to administering alternate assessment should be mandatory regardless of teacher's years of experience.	0	0	0	0	0
25. Less experienced teacher favors the use of alternate assessment.	0	0	0	0	0
26. "Highly qualified" special education teachers are experienced to administer alternate assessments.	0	0	0	0	0
27. Experience influences teacher attitude in administering alternate assessment.	0	0	0	0	0
28. Experience in instruction in academic content standards has a positive influence in administering alternate assessment.	0	0	0	0	0
29. Experience in instruction in academic content standards has a negative influence in administering alternate assessment.	0	0	0	0	0
30. Special education teachers need additional college courses to prepare for administering alternate assessment.	0	0	0	0	0

APPENDIX H

Open-Ended Questionnaire

Section A

Please answer the following questions with as much detail as possible. Use the backside of this questionnaire if necessary to complete your response.

Questionnaire for Teacher Preparation

Please answer the following questions with as much detail as possible.

1. What is the extent of your college experience in preparing you to administer the alternate assessment?
2. Please list what you consider to be the main factor(s) for preparing a teacher toward administering alternate assessment
3. What would you do differently if you were given additional training for administering the alternate assessment?
4. How has your educational preparation influenced your experience in administering alternate assessment?
5. How have opportunities for staff development provided by your school/district met your needs for administering alternate assessment?

6. Approximately how many hours of training have your department/school conducted about alternate assessment in the past year?

Section C

Demographic Information

Directions: Please provide ONE response to each question unless otherwise directed.

1. Gender:

   0 Male   0 Female

2. Please indicate your ethnicity/race.

   0 Asian

   0 American Indian or Alaska Native

   0 Hispanic or Latino

   0 Native Hawaiian or Pacific Islander

   0 White

   0 Black or African American

3. How many years have you taught special education prior to this year?

   0 Less than one year   0 7–9 years

   0 1–3 years   0 10–12 years

   0 4–6 years   0 More than 12 years

4. What is your highest level of education?

0   BA / BS

0   MA / MS

0   Ed.D. / Ph.D.

0   Other

5. Approximately how many complete alternate assessments have you reviewed in the past year?

6. What types of disability categories are used to describe students who participated in the alternate assessment? (Check all that apply)

0   Mild MR   0   Learning Disabilities

0   Traumatic Brain Injury

0   Moderate MR   0   Multiple Disabilities

0   Orthopedic Impairment

0   Severe-Profound MR   0   Behavior/Emotional Disorder

0   Autism   0   Visual/Hearing Impairments

0   Other

7. Do scores from the alternate assessments influence individual school sites' accountability/accreditation status?

0   Yes   0   No   0   Not yet determined

8. What level is your school?

0   Not applicable/ Don't know

0   Elementary   0   Middle

0   High